JOSEPH E. GROSBERG

Supermarket Pioneer of Schenectady

by

Cindy Sabulis

ISBN-13: 978-1-7366065-1-3
Toat Publishing

Foreword

As a teenager in the early 1900s, Joseph Grosberg went into the grocery business with his father, delivering goods to customers around Schenectady, New York by horse and wagon. By the time he was in his 20s, he owned two thriving wholesale grocery businesses, one in Schenectady, the other in Amsterdam, New York. In 1932, Grosberg merged his Schenectady wholesale company with fellow wholesaler Lewis Golub. The newly-formed Grosberg-Golub Company went on to open a chain of supermarkets in the northeast part of the country called Central Markets, the predecessor of Price Chopper Supermarkets and Market 32.

Grosberg was born in Russia and came to the United States as a toddler. From an early age, he took an active role in civic organizations around Schenectady. Jewish affairs were especially of interest to him. Hoping to make life better for the large number of Jewish immigrants flocking into Schenectady, Grosberg helped establish many Jewish organizations in the 1920s and 1930s, and he donated sizable contributions, both in money and time, to aid their efforts. Wherever the greatest need for Jewish aid was needed, Grosberg was there to help. In addition to being a leader and loyal supporter of Jewish programs in and around the Schenectady area, he supported numerous programs that aided Jewish people in Palestine, then later, in the new state of Israel, and war-ridden European countries.

From forming new civic organizations to heading a corporation that launched a chain of supermarkets, Grosberg spent his whole life as a doer. He was a respected businessman, civic leader, and philanthropist. This is an account of his life and the role he played in helping shape the city of Schenectady, New York.

The Grosbergs Come to America

Joseph E. Grosberg was a prominent businessman and Jewish leader in Schenectady, New York. His father, Jacob Grosberg, was born in Goniadz, Russia (later Poland), a village 20 miles southwest of Sztabin, Poland. Jacob's original name was Morris Gans (possible spelling Gantz), a name he later abandoned for Jacob Grosberg. Joseph's mother was Hannah Lasky from Suwalki, Poland. Jacob and Hannah married in 1883 during a time when anti-Jewish riots were cropping up all around Russia and Poland. Czar Alexander II had been assassinated just a couple years prior in 1881. After the czar's assassination, his successor, Alexander III, annulled many of the rights of Jewish people in Russia and a government wave of state-sponsored massacres was launched. Jewish communities in Eastern Europe were targets of state-sponsored murder and destruction, and Jewish villages and neighborhoods were burned by rampaging mobs. Thousands of Jews were slaughtered, both by peasants and by Russian soldiers.

In December of 1883 Jacob and Hannah's first child, Joseph Ezekiel[1], was born in a Russian village called Shtabin[2]. The baby's first name may have originally been Yosef or some other Hebrew, Polish, or Russian derivative of the name Joseph. It is also unknown if the family's surname of Gans/Gantz was changed before Joseph was born or after. An 1887 Castle Garden ship's record for passage to the US believed to be Joseph's lists a three-year-old by the name Josch Grosberg arriving from "Stobin," [sic] Russia. Whether or not Josch was the correct spelling of his name back in Russia cannot be confirmed, but it is the earliest record found for him. If the family's last name was changed after he was born, his original name may have been Josch or Yosef Gans.[3]

In 1885 when Hannah was pregnant with their second child, a plan was set into motion for Jacob to get the family out of Russia. Leaving his pregnant wife and young son Joseph behind, Jacob, along with his wife's brother, Jacob Lasky and some other men from their village, headed for the United States. The group started out on foot towards Germany. At one point they swam through an icy river to avoid Russian border guards and their guard dogs.[4] While the guards were huddled around a fire for warmth, the travelers maneuvered their way through the ice floes without being detected. Either before he left his village, or during his journey out of Russia, Jacob bought some identification papers with the more-German-sounding last name of Grosberg, and that became the name the family went by, abandoning the Gans surname.

When the men reached Hamburg, Germany, they boarded a ship to the United States. They arrived through Castle Garden Emigrant Landing Depot in New York City, and from there Jacob Grosberg headed north to Troy, New York. After securing work and housing in Troy, he sent for his wife, Hannah, and his (now) two young sons to join him in the US.

Jacob paid for cabin class passage for his family on the ship, but at the time, women traveling alone or with small children were often put in steerage—the cheapest and most horrible place to be on a ship--and their cabin class space was sold to someone else. It was a common practice with immigrant ships and one the shipping companies often got away with. When Hannah boarded the ship with 3 ½ year-old Joseph and infant Charles, even though her ticket was for cabin class, she was put in steerage. She could neither read nor write, so probably didn't know her ticket was for better accommodations than what she was given.

When Hannah and her children landed at Castle Garden in New York in August 1887, Jacob was waiting to meet them at the cabin class arrival gate. However, when the cabin class passengers disembarked from the ship, Jacob's family was not among them. Instead, Hannah departed from the steerage gate, only to discover that her husband was not there to meet them. While Hannah sat and worried that she and the children would be sent back to Russia since there was no sponsor to claim her, Jacob hunted all over the crowded immigration center trying to locate them. Eventually he found them, but he was angry when he learned his wife did not receive the cabin-class accommodations he had paid for. After he settled his family in their new home in Troy, he hired a lawyer to write a letter to the president of the Hamburg-America Line Shipping Company, Albert Ballin, to complain about the injustice of forcing his wife to travel in steerage when he had paid for cabin class. In due time, Jacob received an apology letter from the shipping company, along with a full refund for his wife's ticket to the United States.[5]

Over the next decade, Jacob and Hannah, whose first name was Americanized to Anna, had six more US-born children; Myer in 1888, William in 1894, Benjamin in 1896, Harold in 1898, Marion in 1902, and Ruth in 1903.

Jacob and Hannah (Anna) Grosberg circa 1898-1899 with six of their eight children. Front Row: (left to right) William, Harold, Benjamin. Center Row: Hannah & Jacob. Back Row: Charles, Joseph, Myer.
Bellin Family Archives

Early Life in Troy and Schenectady

As the oldest child, Joseph Grosberg began earning money at a young age to help support his family. One of his first jobs as a young boy was selling newspapers on street corners.

Sometime between 1896 and 1900 the Grosbergs moved from Troy to Schenectady. Schenectady was becoming a major economic force with the help of General Electric's headquarters opening there in 1892, so prospects for work and business looked more promising for the Grosbergs than it did in Troy.

From around 1900 to 1912 the Grosbergs owned and operated a small grocery store in Schenectady. It took minimal knowledge of English and little start-up capital to open a corner grocery store in the early 1900s. Consequently, the grocery business attracted many immigrants during this period of time, including the Grosbergs. The Grosberg boys all helped their father in the store as soon as they were old enough, but Joseph, being the oldest, had the most responsibility. Jacob and Anna owned the building at 448 South Centre (Center) Street where their store was located. The family lived in one apartment in the building and they rented out another apartment to tenants.

When they were teenagers, Joseph and his brother Charles decided to branch out from working in the grocery store and started their own business selling shoes.[6] Their inventory consisted of only a limited number of shoes and a whole bunch of empty shoe boxes to make it appear they had a larger inventory than they actually did.
A 1902 Schenectady City Directory lists Anna Grosberg as having shoe stores at her home address and on Albany Street. Possibly, that listing pertained to the shoe business said to be run by her two oldest sons. The shoe business was short-lived for the young entrepreneurs, but it demonstrated the initiative and business drive both Joseph and Charles had from a young age and throughout their careers.

Grosberg Anna Mrs., shoe stores 448 South Centre, 761 Albany, house 448 South Centre
Grosberg Jacob, merchant, house 448 South Centre
Grosberg Joseph E., clerk, boards 448 South Centre

Grosberg listings from the 1902 Schenectady City Directory.

In 1906 when Joseph (Joe) Grosberg was just a couple of months shy of 23, he married 23-year-old Rachel Greenberg. Rae, as she was called, was born in Poland in 1883, about 5 ½ months before Joe. Both Rae and Joe came to the US almost at the same age, within a year or so of each other, and they both lived in Troy during their childhoods. It is believed that the Grosberg and Greenberg families had some personal connection going back to when they lived in Russia/Poland. Both Joe's and Rae's mothers came from the same province of Suwalki in Poland[7], so it's possible their marriage may have been encouraged by the two families.

Joe and Rae Grosberg were married in Troy on October 21, 1906 by Rabbi Hyman M. Lasker. After they married, they lived in Joe's parents' building on South Centre in Schenectady in the extra apartment that was previously rented to tenants and Joe continued working with his father in their grocery store. In 1908, Joe and Rae welcomed their first child, daughter Mildred. In 1912, second daughter Rosalind was born, and a third daughter Marian arrived in 1915.

Joseph (Joe) Grosberg and his wife Rachel (Rae). It is believed this is the couple's wedding portrait, circa 1906. *Bellin Family Archives*

Business Life

By 1911, Joe and his father Jacob were officially business partners. Highly motivated and business-minded, Joe continued to look for new ways to make their grocery store successful. Before long, Jacob took a back seat in the business, allowing Joe to take the lead in driving it. Within a year after incorporating as "Jacob Grosberg and Son," Joe changed the course of their retail grocery store from selling directly to the consumer to selling wholesale to merchants. The Grosberg's wholesale grocery store operated as a cash-and-carry business where merchants came to purchase their own goods rather than the old way of placing orders and having the goods delivered to the merchants' stores. This cut down on delivery costs and allowed store owners to purchase goods at lower prices. Cash and carry also eliminated the problem of extending credit to store owners who were often slow to pay their bills.

Skeptics didn't think cash and carry would work because of the necessity so many merchants had for paying for their goods on credit, but enough of them were willing to pay cash if it meant saving money, so the idea took hold. The change from retail to wholesale groceries turned out to be a good move for the Grosbergs.

In 1913, the Grosbergs moved their wholesale business from their store on South Centre Street to a newly-built warehouse at 47-49 Van Guysling Avenue in Schenectady. The three-story brick building was equipped with an electric freight elevator and steam heat. In addition to the warehouse, there were stables for the horses that were used to transport goods. Later when they began to phase out delivery by horse and wagon, the stables were used as a garage for their company trucks. This larger warehouse was a big step up for the Grosbergs' expanding business.

Jacob Grosberg and Son obtained the rights to be an exclusive area distributor for several products, including Duluth Imperial Flour. The Grosbergs were already carrying Duluth flour at their store on South Centre, but when they moved to Van Guysling, the brick building featured a large advertisement for Duluth Imperial Flour prominently displayed on the building. Newspaper print ads for the flour were run regularly listing Jacob Grosberg and Son as the sole distributor in the Schenectady area, although later on, another area wholesaler shared those Schenectady distributor rights.

The Grosbergs' warehouse on Van Guysling Ave. The sign on the top of the building reads, "Jacob Grosberg & Son," "Grocers" and "Duluth Imperial Flour." *Image from Grems-Doolittle Library Photograph Collection*

Originally the property and warehouse on Van Guysling Avenue was in Jacob and Anna Grosberg's names, but in 1915 they sold it to Joe, along with the building they still owned at 448 South Centre Street. Jacob Grosberg was planning to retire from the grocery business and move out of the Schenectady area. Sometime between 1915 and 1916, Jacob and Anna, along with their six youngest children, moved to Detroit, Michigan. Anna Grosberg's brother, Jacob Lasky, lived in the Detroit area, as did the Grosberg's second-born son, Charles. Charles had visited his Uncle Jacob in Detroit several years prior and while there met a Detroit girl and ended up marrying her.

Charles was settled in Detroit and was running a very successful wholesale grocery business much like his father's and Joe's wholesale company in Schenectady.

After the Grosberg family settled in Detroit, Jacob's intended plan to retire didn't happen right away. Instead, he and his younger sons opened yet another wholesale grocery store in Detroit called J. Grosberg & Son. William, Ben, and Harold all ended up working in the Detroit wholesale grocery business at one time or another.

While his father and brothers made their new mark in Detroit, Joe stayed in Schenectady where he already had made a name for himself. His wholesale business was already well established by this time, plus he was involved in many groups and activities within the Schenectady community. Joe and Rae had three daughters by this time, and his wife had extended family in nearby Troy, including her mother, an aunt and uncle, and cousins who were like siblings to her. Leaving Schenectady to start a new life in Detroit did not make sense for them.

Even after his father was no longer involved in the company, the younger Grosberg continued using the name "Jacob Grosberg and Son" for his Schenectady business. He was always looking for new innovations that would help build and expand his business. He phased out delivery of goods by horse and wagon, updating the process with delivery trucks that could haul more goods more efficiently. When Joe purchased a Ford worm-drive truck, he claimed the distinction of being the very first person in the Schenectady area to own one.

Although Grosberg's wholesale business was doing well, there were some setbacks. Warehouse fires were common in those days, and unfortunately, in 1916 a fire broke out at the Van Guysling Avenue warehouse. The top two floors where food was stored were completely in flames by the time firemen arrived. Fire hoses were run from the roofs of adjoining buildings in an effort to extinguish the large blaze, but by the time the fire was put out, the three-story brick building suffered extensive damage. It was a tough blow for him, but Grosberg vowed to repair the damage and continue business. In due time, the Van Guysling warehouse was back up and running.

Four or five years after his father moved from Schenectady, Grosberg decided to change the name of the business from "Jacob Grosberg and Son" to his own name. On November 24, 1920 Joe incorporated under the new name "Joseph E. Grosberg, Inc." His wife Rae was listed as a principal stockholder of the newly-incorporated company. That same year Grosberg also incorporated a second wholesale grocery business in Amsterdam, New York called "Grosberg Grocery Company, Inc." with business associates George and Samuel Cramer. Joe ran the Schenectady wholesale business, while the Cramer brothers managed the Amsterdam store. Originally both wholesale businesses dealt only in dry goods, but later expanded to include produce. Both businesses were exclusive area distributors of products such as Sweet Life, Jes-so brand foods, and Morning Sip Coffee.

Sugar Incident of 1921

During World War I, there was a severe shortage of sugar around the world. After the war ended, the demand for sugar remained higher than the supply, including in and around the Schenectady area.

With the associated costs of storing, insuring, and transporting the sugar to retail dealers, the profit margin on sugar was very low for wholesalers. In October 1919, a conference between Schenectady Mayor Charles A. Simon and six local wholesale grocery dealers, including Joe Grosberg, met to discuss the sugar shortage in the area. The mayor wanted to know the reasons consumers weren't able to buy enough sugar to satisfy their needs and wanted to know why the wholesalers didn't buy as much sugar as the government allotment allowed them the previous spring. Speculation was that wholesalers had helped create a worse situation by not buying as much sugar as they could prior to the tighter restrictions. The wholesalers denied the claim. Instead, they felt that the local shortage had more to do with hoarding by consumers, primarily housewives, who were buying more sugar than they needed and storing it, fearful that they wouldn't be able to get enough sugar for all their canning and baking needs. The wholesalers also placed the shortage blame on the Sugar Equalization Board's delay in bidding on a recently harvested crop of Cuban sugar that ended up going to Britain instead of the United States.[8]

In June or July of 1920 when sugar demand was still higher than the supply, Grosberg signed a contract with the American Sugar Refining Company for an order of 575 barrels of refined sugar (about 201,250 pounds) at 22 ½ cents a pound. Before he received his shipment, the supply of sugar became more readily available and the price dropped. In 1921 the American Sugar Refining Company delivered the sugar that Grosberg had ordered the previous summer and tried to charge him the previously-agreed-upon price of 22 ½ cents a pound. The going price of sugar at that point was down to 5 cents a pound. Grosberg refused delivery of the sugar and American Sugar Refining sued him for $28,000 for breach of contract.[9]

Because of the lawsuit filed against Grosberg, Schenectady County Supreme Court Justice Charles E. Nickols signed a warrant of attachment against his Van Guysling Avenue property. Grosberg was served the warrant by Sheriff Daniel Manning's office, but on a technicality that the warrant was against Grosberg and not his business he was able to continuing doing business while the lawsuit was being argued.[10]

The lawsuit of American Sugar Refining Company vs. Grosberg was the first incident on record that had been brought to the courts in the Schenectady area where a case based on prices that prevailed during a war retailed at a lesser value after the war. Many wholesale buyers, including Grosberg, placed large orders for sugar when prices were listed at 20 or more cents a pound. When the product became readily available and the price of the previously hard-to-get product dropped, those customers didn't want to pay the old price when it was selling for so much less. The lawsuit filed against Grosberg reflected the nationwide activities of both the American Sugar Refining Company imposing the sugar-shortage prices of their products upon their buyers after the shortage had ended, and of wholesalers refusing to accept delivery.

The American Sugar Refining Company continued to file law suits against their wholesale customers around the country who were refusing delivery of their sugar orders at their much-higher contract prices. Wholesalers tried to argue that the refiner's salesmen had misrepresented sugar market conditions, telling them the price was going to go up to 30 cents a pound and encouraging them to lock in at the 22 ½ cent per pound price while they could. Some defendants used the argument that the sugar company had a supply of sugar on hand sooner, but the company held back delivery longer than necessary, waiting for prices to rise even more. Instead, the price fell. A number of cases that played out in court were found in the sugar company's favor.

The American Sugar Refining Company v. Grosberg case was settled out of court within a week of the lawsuit being filed. It is unknown if Grosberg was forced to pay the entire amount American Sugar Refining was trying to collect from him, but whatever the settled amount was, it was a huge financial loss for him.[11]

Private Label Canned Goods

In 1922, Joseph E. Grosberg, doing business as Grosberg Packing Company, applied for a patent for canned fruits, vegetables, and spices. Grosberg also applied for a logo trademark for the name "Snow Baby." According to US Patent Office information, Grosberg's business had been using the name Snow Baby since 1915. The patent and trademark were issued to him in 1923. A number of stores and restaurants around Schenectady and surrounding towns carried the Snow Baby brand of canned and jar foods, which included corn, peas, tomatoes, olives, sauerkraut, sliced beef, and many others. The label expanded into ammonia, coffee, and ketchup. The Snow Baby label was available for at least the next eight years after it was trademarked, although it may have been sold for much longer.

Ser. No. 170,683. (CLASS 46. FOODS AND INGREDIENTS OF FOODS.) JOSEPH E. GROSBERG, doing business as Grosberg Packing Co., Schenectady, N. Y. Filed Oct. 13, 1922.

SNOW BABY

Particular description of goods.—Canned Fruits, Canned Vegetables, and Spices.

Claims use since 1915.

Logo for Snow Baby brand foods listed in the Official Gazette of the United States Patent Office, Volume 308, 1923, p.683.

Business Expansion

By 1923, Grosberg's Schenectady wholesale business had once again outgrown its facilities. Joseph E. Grosberg, Inc. vacated Van Guysling Avenue, and moved to a new warehouse on Erie Boulevard. Instead of selling the Van Guysling warehouse, Grosberg leased it to various other businesses, including fellow wholesaler and future business partner Lewis Golub.

Erie Boulevard became Grosberg's main business hub. Over the course of four decades, he owned a number of buildings and undeveloped property on Erie Boulevard. Sources have been found that indicate over time he owned 110 Erie Blvd, 130 Erie Blvd, 138-140-142 Erie Blvd, and 271-273 Erie Blvd. His main warehouse for Joseph E. Grosberg, Inc. was located at 130 Erie Blvd. Near his warehouse was a two-story building that was once part of Peckham & Wolf Lumber Company, later headquarters for C.S. Smith Wholesale Grocers. Grosberg purchased that building around 1923 from Charles Smith and renamed it the Grosberg Building. He owned the building for the next 40 years. It was used for office space for himself and his company, and he leased out additional space in the building to other businesses.

In addition to the property and buildings he owned on Erie Boulevard, Grosberg's real estate holdings included buildings all around Schenectady. He leased out entire buildings or divided space to individuals or businesses for stores, offices, or warehouses. He also purchased land around Schenectady, sometimes selling it for profit, sometimes building to suit, then leasing the building.

Grosberg and Golub Wholesalers Merge

By 1926 Lewis Golub was leasing Grosberg's old warehouse at 47-49 Van Guysling Avenue. Golub and Grosberg had known each other for years. In addition to both owning wholesale grocery businesses in Schenectady, they were both involved in many of the same civic and religious organizations. At some point, presumably around 1930, Lewis Golub became ill and went to Europe to try to recuperate while his sons William and Bernard, both in their 20s, ran their father's wholesale business.

Three months before his death, Golub returned to the US, perhaps to settle his affairs. It is unknown which businessman first approached the other about merging their two companies, but it's been stated in many newspaper articles that Lewis Golub wanted to leave behind a legacy for his sons to become a part of a larger, stronger company when he merged his business with Grosberg's. Grosberg's two wholesale businesses were firmly established and doing well at that point, and his many real estate investments put him in a solid financial position. If Golub was looking for a chance to secure his sons' futures and Grosberg was looking for an opportunity to further expand his business, a merger between the two wholesalers looked like a promising opportunity for both. The merger between Golub Cash & Carry Wholesale Groceries and Joseph E. Grosberg, Inc. took place February 1930, just a week before Lewis Golub succumbed to cancer. The merger did not include Grosberg's second wholesale business in Amsterdam, NY. Grosberg Grocery Company in Amsterdam remained a separate business and continued under the management of Grosberg's business partners George and Samuel Cramer.

Because the value of Grosberg's Schenectady wholesale business was more substantial than Golub's and due to the fact that Grosberg had more experience in the wholesale business than did Lewis Golub's two sons, the Grosberg/Golub merger was weighted in Grosberg's favor. Under the terms of the merger, Grosberg maintained a larger share of the company and was named president. Lewis's son William (Bill) Golub was named vice president and his brother Bernard (Ben) Golub was treasurer. Rae Grosberg, who was listed on record as secretary for her husband's business prior to the merger, was again listed as the company's secretary. Nathan Levine, who had been working as a salesman for Grosberg for many years and was married to Rae's cousin, Mary Greenblath, became assistant treasurer of the company.

Initially, the name of the Grosberg/Golub newly-merged company was Double GG Grocery Company, Inc. Immediately following the merger, the Golub brothers moved their business out of the Van Guysling Avenue warehouse they were leasing from Grosberg to Grosberg's larger warehouse on Erie Boulevard.

Municipal Grocery Stores, Inc.

Less than a month after the merger with the Golubs, Grosberg was spearheading a movement to bring chapters of Municipal Grocery Stores both to Schenectady and Amsterdam. Municipal Grocery Stores, Inc. of New York City was a voluntary cooperative organization of independently-owned grocers. At the time, chain stores were sprouting up around the country and the independent grocer was having difficulties competing. By banding together, the small grocers, in a way, created their own small chain, thus allowing them to better compete with larger chains. With the backing of Municipal Grocery Stores, Inc., small grocers gained increased buying power and were able to purchase goods at lower prices. Members of the group shared co-operative advertising, set uniform prices, and had a centralized direction of store policies. Members also had access to merchandising experts who were available for advice about the industry.

The Schenectady chapter of Municipal Grocery Stores started with 30 independently-owned retail grocery stores signing up. Each grocer belonging to Municipal Grocery Stores had a uniformed orange and green store front, signs with gold lettering, and a uniformed interior to distinguish them as members of the chain. Big gold signs were placed in their store windows promising economy, quality, and personal service. Modern accounting and auditing systems were installed to help eliminate the old-fashioned effort of trying to determine profit. To help bring in business for their members, Municipal Grocery Stores ran large advertisements in local papers.

By May of 1930, Grosberg was vice-president of the Schenectady chapter of Municipal Grocery Stores and Bernard Golub was secretary.[12] Grosberg and the Golub brothers designated nearly 40,000 square feet of space at the rear of their warehouse at 140 Erie Blvd for Municipal Grocery Stores to use as offices and to store and distribute goods.

While Grosberg worked to help build up the Schenectady chapter of Municipal Grocery Stores, his Amsterdam partners, the Cramer brothers, built up the Amsterdam chapter. Grosberg Grocery in Amsterdam was the sponsoring company for the chapter in that city.[13]

As the area Municipal Grocery Stores grew in numbers, they began sponsoring family outings and sports teams. Contests at Municipal stores were held and prizes awarded. The first food show in Amsterdam sponsored by the Municipal Grocery Stores took place in January 1931 and drew 20,000 people. $319 of cash sales was donated to a community Welfare Fund.[14] Other promotional offers and events were held to entice customers to shop at Municipal Grocery Stores, including one in June of 1931 when they ran a promotion for a free ticket to the Rialto Theater in Amsterdam with any $1.00 purchase from any participating store.

It may be wondered why Grosberg, who was in the wholesale grocery business, worked so hard to band together independent retail grocers to compete with chain stores. As a wholesaler, it was in his best interest to help his retail grocer customers stay in business. Also, as the sponsoring organization for both Schenectady's and Amsterdam's Municipal Grocery Stores, Grosberg's wholesale businesses benefited by being able to purchase goods in greater quantity at lower prices, and then they were able to pass on those lower prices to their customers, the retail grocer. The more retail grocers who signed into the Municipal Grocery Stores cooperative, the more customers it meant for Grosberg's two wholesale businesses, Double GG Grocery and Grosberg Grocery. In addition to the built-in customer base it offered him, Municipal Grocery Stores began carrying Grosberg's private label Snow Baby canned vegetables. Municipal Grocery Stores also carried Sweet Life products, a national brand that Grosberg's two wholesale food companies were exclusive area distributors for.

Central Markets

In January 1931, eleven months after the merger of Grosberg's and Golub's wholesale companies, Double GG Grocery Company, Inc. changed its name to Grosberg-Golub Company, Inc. Around this same time, Grosberg-Golub began to change the direction of their business as well. Although they were in the process of trying to band together independent grocers so they could compete against chain stores, the Grosberg-Golub owners started laying the groundwork to open their own supermarket that would eventually go on to become a chain of stores.

The Grosberg-Golub partners leased an empty warehouse at Paine and Swan Streets in the Green Island part of Troy for their first supermarket. The building was owned by Hugh R. McCarney, an experienced grocer who had sold his own grocery chain of 55 stores to Grand Union. McCarney was put in charge of managing the operation for the new store. He began leasing departments for the proposed supermarket to independent vendors. Space in the store was rented to a butcher for meat, a green grocer for produce, and a baker for breads, cakes, and other baked goods. A jeweler, a barber, an antique dealer, a bookseller, a tailor, and a shoe repairman also leased space in the store. It wasn't just a food market, it was a "*Super* Market" that contained over 30 different vendors selling everything from women's clothing to household furniture. Each vendor who signed on built their own booth within the store and supplied the goods for it.

As opening day for the new supermarket neared, doubts about whether or not the public would come starting taking hold. It was even suggested by one of the Golub brothers that they keep all the cartons the groceries came in so in the event things didn't sell, they had the cartons to repack it all.

The new Grosberg-Golub supermarket opened on November 17, 1932. Most written references on the history of Central Markets indicate that the first store was originally called the *Public Service Market*. However, many advertisements from 1933 and 1934 called the store the *Public Service Economy Market.* At least one ad in 1933 called it the *Public Service Economy Center*. William Golub, when interviewed for Maxwell Zimmerman's book The Super Market; A Revolution in Distribution published in 1955 called it the *Public Service Center*. The company filed a new corporation in May 23, 1933 under the name *Public Service Center, Inc.*

The Public Service Market (a/k/a Public Service Economy Market/Center) was the first self-serve supermarket in the Troy, New York area. Initially, skeptics felt the lack of personalized service wouldn't appeal to consumers. As it turned out, customers didn't mind less individualized attention if it meant savings. The Public Service Market's emphasis on low prices turned out to be very successful in the Depression-era economy. Consumers flocked to the new store that sold goods at wholesale prices to the retail market. In addition to the low prices, part of the appeal was that customers could make selections without being hurried or influenced by a clerk as sometimes happened in the small "Mom & Pop" stores. Even though the store was touted as being self-serve, the new supermarket store still provided quite a bit of helpful service to customers by clerks, butchers, bakers, and cashiers.

The displays and paying methods of the first Public Service Market were crude by today's standards. Boards placed across sawhorses held merchandise stacked on and below them, and bins of goods lined aisles. Customers carried their groceries in wicker baskets, since shopping carts on wheels hadn't yet been thought of. When customers were ready to check out, they headed to a stand in the middle of the store where clerks tallied up their orders on adding machines. The clerks gave each customer a slip with their total. The customer then took the slip to a cashier to pay. After getting a stamped receipt from the cashier the customer went back to the clerk to get their groceries. Later this system was redesigned to make the checkout process simpler.

Even before witnessing the full success of the first Public Service Market, Grosberg and the Golubs were planning additional supermarket stores. Within a few months, a second Public Service Market opened on Broadway in Watervliet, NY. Grosberg-Golub, Inc. opened a third store at 1639 Eastern Parkway in Schenectady in August 1933, less than a year after opening their first store. The building for the third store was in a vacated automobile dealer's sales and service garage previously used by Hupmobile. It was decided that the name of this new supermarket store would be Central Market based on the close proximity to that city's Central Park. It was also decided to change the name of the first two stores from Public Service Market to Central Market.

Hugh McCarney was again put in charge of operations for the new Schenectady store. Prior to the store's opening, the company targeted advertising to housewives, promising them sanitary facilities, lower prices, as well as more and better selection of merchandise. When the grand opening of the third Central Market store took place, it was met with crowds of people. As quickly as merchandise was purchased by customers, it was restocked by the workers. Grosberg and the Golub brothers were on to something big. Supermarkets with their emphasis on low prices were more popular than the small corner store that offered shoppers more personalized service at a higher price.

Central Market's policy was "high quality plus low price equals real value." Providing food to the public at the lowest possible cost was accomplished through the company's tremendous buying power, selling in large volumes, and low overhead in the operation of the big supermarket.[15] Central Markets kept their margin of profit low for each item they sold, in return for the large volume of sales it brought in.

Another appeal to customers was that Central Markets implemented "the customer is always right" rule, and every item sold in their stores was unconditionally guaranteed. If an item was returned, it was readily exchanged for another, or the customer's money refunded.

While many vendors who leased space in the stores made enough sales to turn a profit, not all of them were able to ride the wave of Central Market's success. Due to the fact that the country was in the Great Depression, some of the vendors who signed up to sell their wares in the supermarket operated on limited budgets and didn't survive very long. One such department--dry goods--was about to close out when one of Grosberg-Golub's employees with extensive experience in the dry goods field suggested the company try operating that department on their own.[16] With that suggestion, Central Markets took over their own operations of dry goods and non-foods sold in the stores.

Prior to the merger with the Golubs, Grosberg was the exclusive area distributor for Sweet Life and Jes-so brand products through his two wholesale grocery businesses. After the merger, Grosberg-Golub's wholesale company continued as exclusive Schenectady area distributor for those brands, and subsequently, Central Markets took over the role. In addition to canned items, Central Market started carrying frozen foods. When Central Market first started selling Birds Eye brand frozen peas, the produce manager, Henry Diamond, didn't believe anyone would pay the price for frozen peas when the store already had plenty of fresh peas available to customers. Yet, frozen peas and other frozen vegetables became very popular with Central Market shoppers.

On March 30, 1934 a second Schenectady Central Market store opened at 2600 Guilderland Ave, on the corner of Laura Street. This store was referred to as the Bellevue branch store, while the Eastern Parkway store was considered the main Schenectady store. A third Schenectady Central Market opened around May of 1938 at 225-228 Broadway. That store included a dry goods department that sold clothing items such as skirts, dresses, stockings, sheets, and aprons. Because of its location, parking was one block down at Neil F. Ryan's Garage. Patrons needed to tell the garage they were a Central Market customer and get a ticket that would be stamped at the store.

Bulk buying for Central Markets was mostly done through Seaboard Food (Service) Corporation, switching from Municipal Grocery Stores, Inc. Headquartered in New York City, Seaboard Food Corporation was a national organization which consisted of larger supermarket chains working together the same way the small, independent grocers banded together through Municipal Grocery Stores, Inc. The tremendous buying power of Seaboard Food allowed Central Markets to keep their prices low. Like he had done with Municipal Grocery Stores, Grosberg helped found the area's first chapter of Seaboard Food. In 1935 he was Executive Vice President of the national organization and actively serving as a member of the executive committee. In 1936 at the Seaboard Food convention Grosberg was elected President of the organization. While Central Markets did their bulk buying through Seaboard Food, Grosberg's independent Amsterdam wholesale business continued to do their bulk buying through Municipal Grocery Stores, Inc.

In 1935 after Central Market had grown to four or five stores, an article appeared in the January 17 issue of *The Schenectady Gazette* about a new supermarket that was about to open. The article read, "Announcement of the incorporation of Super-Markets, Inc., a new Schenectady firm headed by Joseph E. Grosberg, which plans to convert the former Weidman property, also known as the old Cluett-Peabody factory at Broadway and Hamilton Street, into a mammoth food market was made last night by Harold E. Blodgett of the firm of Blodgett and Smith, attorneys for the concern."[17]

According to the newspaper announcement, the new corporation was formed to engage in a general meat and grocery business. The article stated that organizer and principal subscribers included Joseph Grosberg, Elizabeth V. Lucas (who lived on the same street as Grosberg), and Attorney Howard Murrin of 52 Vley Road, Scotia. It went on to say that a project allied with Super-Markets, Inc. was Central Fruits Company, Inc. which was to engage in fruit and vegetable concessions with the newly-created Super-Markets, Inc. The stockholders for Central Fruits were the same as those of Super-Markets, Inc. except that Henry Diamond was a stockholder instead of Grosberg. Henry Diamond, who headed Central Fruits, was also the manager of the produce department of Central Markets for ten years up until his death in 1944.

The planned store was originally expected to open for business about April 1 but didn't open until the fall of that year. In September 1935 the supermarket at Broadway and Hamilton opened. On September 7, 1935, the *Schenectady Gazette* featured a large photo showing the Super-Markets, Inc. store and said it was opened under the personal direction and management of Joseph Grosberg, president of Grosberg-Golub Company Inc. The short article with the photo discussed the policy of keeping prices down using the Seaboard Food Service, which Grosberg was vice president of at the time.[18] Other than those initial newspaper announcements, there was no more public mention of Grosberg's involvement with that supermarket, or of Central Market's produce manager Henry Diamond or any "Central Fruits" connection. All other references located about Super-Markets, Inc. listed Max Cohn as the founder, owner, or "active head." Although credited as the founder and owner of the store in every other newspaper reference, Cohn was not listed as one of the principal subscribers in the 1935 news announcement of Super-Markets, Inc. being formed, nor in the announcement of the store opening in September 1935.

In spite of Grosberg's name being mentioned in a couple of newspaper articles stating his involvement in Super-Markets, Inc., a Central Market full-page advertisement in 1936 printed a small disclaimer at the top right-hand corner stating, "*False Rumor! Central Markets Have Absolutely no connection Whatsoever With Any Other Market in Schenectady.*"[19] Even though Central Markets might not have been connected to Super-Markets, Inc., Grosberg may have been, at least for a little while. The newspaper article that stated Grosberg was a principal subscriber and a second article that mentioned the store was opened "under the personal direction and management of Joseph Grosberg, president of Grosberg-Golub" do not sound like simple newspaper errors. It's possible Grosberg was involved with initially setting up the corporation and supermarket then sold it off to Max Cohn, but at the time of this writing, no proof other than those two news stories have been uncovered to learn if Grosberg was involved in Super-Markets, Inc. Max Cohn was a member of Congregation Agudas Achim for 50 years, the same synagogue Grosberg was heavily involved in. Cohn was a member of Agudas Achim's board of directors for 25 years and president of the congregation for 15 years. He was one of the organizers of the Supermarket Institute and an Elks member. Grosberg was involved in all of these activities as well, so Cohn and Grosberg traveled in many of the same circles and must have been well acquainted with each other. Whether or not they had some kind of early business deal relating to Super-Markets, Inc. has yet to be confirmed.

As for Central Markets, they expanded rapidly. Within six years after opening the first Central Market store in Green Island, Grosberg and the Golub brothers had nine

Central Market stores in operation in or around the Capital region of New York. By 1938, Central Markets employed more than 500 people.

William and Bernard Golub with Joseph Grosberg in front of one of the Central Market stores on opening day. The store is believed to be the Madison and Swan store in Albany, which opened in February 1941. *Bellin Family Archives*

Central Market store grand opening. It is believed this was the Central Market located at the corner of Madison Avenue and Swan in Albany, which would date it to February 1941. *Bellin Family Archives*

Over the next decade, Central Market stores were opened in North Troy, Glens Falls, and Albany. Central Markets became one of the largest and fastest growing chains of supermarkets in the area. Helping in Central Markets' growth was newspaper and radio advertising. Twice a day on WGY (NBC) radio in Schenectady were five-minute talks called, "The Voice of the Central Markets," conducted by Lois Carroll. Carroll presented listeners with the latest food values at Central Market stores. In 1941 radio commentator Col. Jim Healey was added as a spokesperson on WTRY in Troy.

Joseph Grosberg visiting the Sweet Life canning factory in California, 1937. *Bellin Family Archives*

In 1943, after more than 40 years in the grocery business, Grosberg decided it was time to retire, so he sold his shares of Grosberg-Golub, Inc. and Central Markets to the Golub brothers. The newly-renamed Golub Corporation stayed at 140 Erie Blvd in the Grosberg Building, leasing warehouse and office space from Grosberg up until the early 1960s

William Golub and Joseph Grosberg, July 1938.
Photo courtesy of Marsha Axler

Grosberg Grocery, Amsterdam, NY

During the years that Grosberg was building up his Schenectady wholesale business, as well as during the period when he was starting up Central Markets, his Amsterdam wholesale business, Grosberg Grocery, was run under the management of brothers, Sam and George Cramer. The Cramers were original stockholders in the 1920 formation of Grosberg Grocery, with Grosberg the principal stockholder. At first, the Amsterdam wholesale business was located on Schuyler Street, but on September 17, 1923, the company moved their offices and warehouses to 152-160 West Main Street, Amsterdam. Although Grosberg lent his well-known name and financial backing to the Amsterdam wholesale store, by all appearances, it seemed he was primarily a silent partner in the day-to-day operation.

In September 1932, just a month before the first Central Market store opened, Grosberg and the Cramer brothers incorporated again under the new name Grosberg-Cramer Company, Inc. Since the Amsterdam wholesale grocery business was now carrying the Cramer name, Sam and George may have become equal financial partners with Grosberg in the business at that point, or maybe they took over a bigger share of the company. In spite of the use of his name in the business name, Grosberg was not listed in a newspaper legal notice as being one of the principal shareholders of Grosberg-Cramer Company. At some point, the Cramer brothers started using the name S. & G. Cramer Company. In 1940, a few months after George Cramer's death, Sam Cramer filed a legal motion to continue using the name S. & G. Cramer Company, running the business on his own. Logically, it seems that Grosberg was no longer involved in the Amsterdam business at that point, however, three years later in 1943 when Grosberg announced his retirement from the grocery business, a legal notice in the paper in November of that year indicated the corporate title of Grosberg Grocery Company in Amsterdam (not the Grosberg-Cramer Company) had been changed to S. & G. Cramer, Inc. If Grosberg had already sold out his share of the business to the Cramers prior to that, and the brothers were already using the name S. & G. Cramer, the official filing of the name change in 1943 may have been a technically that had been overlooked earlier.

Joseph Grosberg and Samuel Cramer with a Grosberg Grocery Company truck, circa early 1920s. *Bellin Family Archives*

A delivery truck marked, "Grosberg Wholesale Grocer," circa early 1920s. *Bellin Family Archives*

Life After Central Markets and Grosberg Grocery

Grosberg was just a few months shy of 60 years old when he decided to retire from the grocery business in 1943. After stepping down as head of Central Markets, he remained active in civic and charitable organizations and continued investing in real estate around the Schenectady area, buying up real estate on his own, or partnering with other businessmen who were long-time acquaintances.

In June of 1945, two years after he retired from Central Markets and the wholesale grocery industry, Grosberg, along with his wife's nephew, Hyman Cooper, purchased a department store in Burlington, Vermont. Frank's Economy Store, previously owned by father and son Barnet and Belmont Frank, was one of the leading retail establishments in the Burlington area at the time of the sale. Grosberg may have been a silent partner in the purchase of this Vermont store, thinking of it as another investment opportunity, or perhaps he was just helping his wife's nephew by loaning him the startup money. Several newspaper accounts of the sale listed both Grosberg and Cooper as the buyers of the store, however, after the initial purchase of Frank's Economy Store, Grosberg's name no longer appeared in any publicity capacity for the store. By October 1945, Hyman, who was also the president of a real estate holding company called Cooper Realty Inc, issued stock for Frank's Economy Store. In the March 6, 1946 issue of Burlington Daily News, Hyman's brother Morris Cooper, who was vice-president of the Cooper Realty real estate holding company, was listed as president of Frank's Economy Store, while Hyman was listed as the treasurer of the store. It's possible the newspaper got the two brothers' names mixed up in their roles. Morris was also named manager of the Burlington store. At one point, Grosberg's son-in-law, Mortimer H. Cohen, was also listed as a vice president.

In his private life, Grosberg purchased a relatively modest-size brick ranch house in the Niskayuna section of Schenectady sometime around 1949. He and his wife Rae divided their time living in Schenectady for part of the year and in Miami Beach, Florida for the other part. Grosberg enjoyed traveling, so he did so as much as he was able, whether it was car trips around the country, or transatlantic cruises to foreign lands. He and his wife often vacationed in the Borscht Belt part of the Catskill

Mountains in New York, and spent many Jewish holidays with groups of friends at legendary resorts like the Concord Hotel.

Among Grosberg's talents was a great aptitude for building and inventing things, as well as fixing broken items to bring them back to life. When he was a young man, he once helped build a house from scratch. That experience taught him skills like construction, carpentry, and electrical wiring. He had an interest in gardening and had a green thumb like his mother Anna. Grosberg read extensively and his house was always filled with books and magazines. It was said he would buy up entire libraries at estate sales. In his younger days, his father taught him religious studies, so he had a strong background in religion. He spoke both Hebrew and Yiddish, as well as English. It is unknown for sure how much formal education Grosberg had. In an interview, one of his daughters stated that she thought her father's schooling stopped after 6th grade, after which time he worked full time to help his father support their family.[20] Other family members thought his education went up to 8th grade, and still others thought he got his high school diploma at night school while he was working, but so far, no concrete proof has turned up to support any of these stories. Although his formal schooling may have ended early, Grosberg's self-taught education continued throughout his life.

Golf was one of Grosberg's free-time passions, and he enjoyed golfing while down in Miami, as well as around the Schenectady area. In his later life, spending time with his ten great-grandchildren was a joy for him. He rarely arrived for a visit with them empty handed, often showing up with a watermelon, rock candy, or some other treat. He'd spend his visits giving piggy back rides to the children and playing games with them that he made up.

In the summer of 1970 while down in Miami Beach, Grosberg broke his hip. While in the hospital, he developed sepsis and passed away on July 25, 1970 at the age of 86. As a well-known business man, his death was reported in many of the upstate New York newspapers. The *New York Times* picked up the story, as did many newspapers around the country.

Rae and Joe Grosberg in Miami Beach, Florida, date unknown.
Bellin Family Archives

After Grosberg's death, his wife Rae lived for a short time with her middle daughter Rosalind, then spent the last six months of her life in the Jewish Home for the Aged in Troy, NY, a place that she and her husband helped found. While living at the Jewish Home for the Aged, Rae took up new hobbies like painting, ceramics, and needlecrafts. She lived to be 88 years old, passing away the following year after her husband on November 9, 1971.

Community Involvement - Religious, Professional, and Civic

Joseph Grosberg spent his entire life building up his businesses, as well as working for and supporting organizations that aided Jewish people in Schenectady and around the world. He had a soft spot for children, and many of the activities he was involved in benefited youth, including the YMHA, the YMCA, and the Kiwanis Club's summer camp. He was a very generous person, both with his time and his money. The work he did during his lifetime set the foundation for many organizations that are still in existence today.

Joe Grosberg, date unknown.
Bellin Family Archives

Some of the organizations Grosberg was involved with or worked to help establish are listed below. This is, by no means, a complete list.

Jewish Organizations and Causes

Between the late 1800s and early 1900s, Jews from Central and Eastern Europe were arriving in Schenectady in large numbers. As the Jewish population increased, newly-formed Jewish organizations began emerging around the area and Grosberg was instrumental in helping to form many of them. Grosberg's deeply-religious father Jacob helped instilled a strong religious commitment in him, and with that came a strong desire to help develop and support Jewish organizations.

The Hebrew Institute of Schenectady was one group Grosberg was strongly committed to. Formed in 1912, the Hebrew Institute helped give boys of modest backgrounds an elementary education in Hebrew, the Scriptures, and the Talmud. In addition to being one of the founders of the Hebrew Institute, Grosberg served as president of the organization from the start. The Institute was located at 504 Hamilton Street in Schenectady, sharing space in the building with the Schenectady Hebrew School Association which had formed a year earlier. The Hebrew Institute not only provided classes for Jewish boys, it became a gathering place for clubs, meetings, and social events for the Jewish community. Beginning as early as 1914, the Institute was trying to raise funds to help those in Palestine and European countries afflicted by war.

One club that met at the United Hebrew Community building was the Junior Welfare League which was dedicated to helping improve the quality of life of the Schenectady community. Grosberg was an advisor for that group.

Closely tied with the Hebrew Institute was another Jewish group, the Young Men's Hebrew Association (YMHA). Grosberg, along with a group of other prominent Jewish men in the city, founded the Schenectady branch of the YMHA around 1916. Because different independent Jewish organizations around Schenectady started offering many of the same programs, they ultimately ended up competing against one another. The purpose of the Young Men's Hebrew Association was to try to centralize the Schenectady Jewish community and help eliminate all the various Jewish groups from acting independently of one another and inadvertently offering the same programs. Smaller Jewish social and sporting groups joined forces and merged into the larger, newly-formed YMHA group, including the Schenectady Apollo Club (also called the Apollo Club or the Schenectady Club), and the Young Maccabees. When the initial steps were taken to organize the YMHA, more than 100 members signed up to join.

The new group represented all brands of Judaism: Orthodox, Conservative, and Reformed. Grosberg was one of the directors of the YMHA.

A year after the formation of the YMHA, a similar group for girls, the Young Women's Hebrew Association (YWHA), was organized. Grosberg, like he had done with so many other organizations, served on the board of directors and was chairman of the welfare board for the group.

By 1923 the Hebrew Institute had outgrown their building on Hamilton Street and moved to a larger building on Albany Street. At that point, the Hebrew Institute became the United Hebrew Community, with Grosberg continuing on as president of the organization. When the United Hebrew Community first incorporated, the plan was to have 25 members on the board of directors. Their mission was to "do charitable work, to improve the spiritual, mental, and social condition of the people of the Jewish faith of the City and County of Schenectady, State of New York."[21] In 1924, Grosberg and the United Hebrew Community were laying out plans for YMHA to also move to the Albany Street site in order to centralize the Jewish community.

By 1926 the United Hebrew Community, the YMHA and YWHA, and Zion Lodge Independent Order of Odd Fellows (I.O.O.F.) put into action a plan to erect a building that would house all the organizations. The Albany Street location expanded to Germania Avenue.

The YMHA and YMHA of Schenectady eventually merged with Schenectady's United Hebrew Community, becoming the Jewish Community Center (JCC) of Schenectady. Grosberg was the first president of the Schenectady Jewish Community Center, which, in the early years, was often called by its former name, the United Hebrew Community. Grosberg remained president until 1930, but his service to the JCC didn't end there. He continued on as Chairman of the Board of Directors/Chairman of the Board of Trustees and served on many committees as the need arose.

In May 1941 a purchase of the property at 302 Germania Avenue by the Jewish Community Center was made possible thanks to a financial gift from Grosberg.[22] Grosberg donated the funds necessary for the JCC to purchase the property for $1,700 after it was put up for sale by the city for back taxes. He also financed the job of converting the property into additional space for the Center. Grosberg offered the JCC free use of a building he owned on the Germania Avenue property. The building was called the Grosberg Building. It hasn't yet been verified if the Grosberg Building was built on the original JCC property, if it was on the property that the JCC purchased with funds donated by Grosberg, or if it was a separate parcel of land on Germania Avenue that Grosberg purchased himself.

In 1957, Grosberg decided that he did not want the Jewish Community Center to be bound by the restrictions that were on the deed to the Grosberg Building so he signed the deed over to the organization with the request that in the event it was necessary to ever sell the building, the money from the sale should be used towards the purchase of a new building.[23] In November 1957 the *Schenectady Gazette* featured a picture of Grosberg turning over the deed to the building to the JCC.

Altogether, Grosberg devoted more than 50 years of service to the Jewish Community Center of Schenectady. He was credited with the early success of the United Hebrew Community and was instrumental in the adaptation of the organization into the Jewish Community Center. The portrait of Grosberg that hangs in the Schenectady Jewish Community Center lists the year he first became president as being 1915.

Photo courtesy of Schenectady Jewish Community Center

However, taking into account his role as president of the Hebrew Institute of Schenectady starting in 1912 (which became the United Hebrew Community in 1923) Grosberg's service as president of the organization could be said to have begun in 1912.

During the time he served as president of the Hebrew Institute and the Jewish Community Center, Grosberg supported the development of the Jewish Social Service Organization (JSSO), a women's group that aided local Jewish individuals or families who needed help. Grosberg's wife Rae was one of the founders of the JSSO. Obviously, Grosberg wasn't a member of this women's group, but every year, for over 51 years, Grosberg installed the officers of the organization.

In addition to his local involvement with the Jewish Community Center, Grosberg served as an officer for the New York State Federation of Young Men's and Women's Hebrew Associations and Jewish Communal Centers.

Grosberg was genuinely invested in the growth and development of Palestine becoming the national homeland for Jewish people of all nations. He was one of the founding members of the *Moriah Zionist Association*, one of the earliest Zionist groups in Schenectady. Although Grosberg's obituary states he helped found the group in 1903, it is believed the group actually started in 1913.

In the early years, Grosberg was the Grand Master for the Zionist group. Funds raised by the Zionists were used for buying and developing land in Palestine for Jewish people. It is unknown how long Grosberg stayed involved with the Moriah Zionists. He was honorary chair in 1931 and was still with the group in 1947. It's likely he stayed involved with the group up until his retirement years, possibly until the end of his life.

In 1916 Grosberg chaired a committee to help jumpstart the Schenectady area's participation in the American Jewish Congress. The American Jewish Congress was a national organization that addressed issues of crucial concern to the Jewish community and other minority civil rights, both in the US and around the world. The Congress Committee in Schenectady had been inactive for some time up to that point. The committee nominated Grosberg to run for election as Congressman to the American Jewish Congress. If elected, he would represent the Schenectady district at a convention in Washington. Grosberg's opponent was Rabbi Joseph Jasin. Well known among the Jewish working population, Rabbi Jasin was officially endorsed by the National Jewish Worker's Alliance of America. In May of 1917, in spite of not being able to campaign too much due to an illness, Rabbi Jasin still beat the younger Grosberg in the election. In 1923 Grosberg was again nominated against six other candidates for a chance for the American Jewish Congress, but later he withdrew from the election.

Another title Grosberg held for at least 21 years was chairman of The United Palestine Appeal/United Jewish Appeal. The United Jewish Appeal (UJA), later called Jewish National Appeal, was a nation-wide campaign to raise funds on behalf of Jews around the world. The organization was devoted to aiding war sufferers and refugees, primarily in Europe, as well as immigration and resettlement of Jews in Palestine/Israel and other overseas places. Grosberg strongly believed in the program, and he worked endlessly chairing campaigns to raise money for the cause. He spoke to Jewish groups all around Schenectady as well as to other chapters of UJA to help get more people involved. Grosberg was especially active in the big gifts division, helping to raise thousands of dollars to assist Jews most in need. During WWII, funds raised by the UJA helped thousands of refugees who were being oppressed and driven from their homes by Hitler, and fleeing Germany for various European countries. After WWII, funds raised by the group continued to help Jewish refugees seeking to establish themselves in Palestine and other regions.

In addition to chairing the Schenectady chapter, Grosberg was elected honorary national vice chairman of the United Palestine Appel in 1938 and served as Regional Vice Chairman of the eastern section of New York in 1940.

Grosberg was a long-time member of the Agudas Achim Synagogue in Schenectady. Agudas Achim, a Hebrew name meaning "a gathering of brothers," later changed to Agudat Achim in following the modern Israeli Hebrew pronunciation of the letter "taf." In 1923, Grosberg served as president of the synagogue, which was often referred to as the Nott Terrace Synagogue. After his first year as president, he took a short break from the role, then took the office again on and off, from 1929 through 1937. Agudas Achim was originally an Orthodox Congregation, but under Grosberg's leadership they changed their affiliation to Conservative. While president, Grosberg helped to organize the creation of the Sisterhood of the Congregation Agudas Achim. Grosberg also served on the board of governors of the synagogue for many years.

Grosberg served as president of the New York Capital District Region of the United Synagogue of America, a laymen's organization for Conservative Judaism. Grosberg was president of the regional group in 1932 and 1933. This group's focus was to help strengthen Jewish life around the Capital district, as well as protest against discrimination and persecution of Jews in various European countries.

In the 1940s, Grosberg served as Regional Vice Chairman for Eastern New York for The American Jewish Joint Committee. The group was a national organization that helped raise funds for food and shelter for Jewish refugees who were forced from their homes in Poland, Germany, and other countries.

Grosberg was a long-time member of the Schenectady Lodge of B'nai B'rith, a Jewish service club which sponsored various Jewish community projects and philanthropies. Grosberg was also a trustee of the group.

Other groups Grosberg was affiliated with included the Council of Jewish Federations and Welfare Funds and the National Council on Jewish Relief, the major American agency for aid to distressed Jews overseas.

Professional Organizations

In the 1930s there were no industry standards or models to influence or guide supermarket owners. In May of 1937, a small group of supermarket owners gathered in the office of Max M. Zimmerman, Super Market Merchandising magazine editor, to discuss the possibility of integrating supermarket owners into a united body. Grosberg was one of the supermarket owners at that meeting. The group discussed the possibility of forming a new organization to unite the supermarket industry, and also to host a convention for people in the industry. This new organization became the Super Market Institute. Grosberg was one of the pioneering leaders of that group and was on the organization committee to help plan the first convention. The group quickly grew to over 200 owners of supermarkets including Grosberg and his Central Markets partner, William Golub. In September 1937, the first Super Market Institute's convention of supermarket operators was held at the Hotel Astor in New York City. Over 1,000 people were in attendance comprising of many different sectors of the food distribution industry from all over the country. Most of the attendees at the convention had never met one another before. While some of them were small operators at the time, many went on to become the most important men in the supermarket industry. At that first convention of the Super Market Institute, Grosberg was elected national recording secretary. [24]

Grosberg and the other men who formed the Super Market Institute were instrumental in charting the early development of the supermarket industry. Today the organization is known as The Food Marketing Institute and consists of members from over 40,000 retail food stores and 25,000 pharmacies.

The Seaboard Food Service was a national wholesale buying organization made up of wholesale grocers located throughout the eastern part of the US. Grosberg was one of the founders of the group, and a member of the executive committee. At the group's 1936 convention, he took office as president of the national organization.

Grosberg was also an officer in the trade organization The New York Wholesale Grocers Association.

Civic and Fraternal Groups

Grosberg was one of 90 charter members of the Schenectady Kiwanis Club when it was first formed in 1919. One of the main activities of the fraternal organization was supporting activities and services for underprivileged children. Funds raised by the Kiwanis Club was used for activities such as sending kids to summer camp, taking groups of kids to the movies or theater, holding Christmas parties for children, and paying the costs of transporting children with cerebral palsy to and from school. The Kiwanis Club organized dental clinics for children whose parents couldn't afford it, they sponsored sewing classes for girls, baseball leagues for kids, outings for underprivileged youths, sponsored events at Boys' Clubs…the list goes on and on. Many of the Kiwanians donated their services to underprivileged kids—such as a Kiwanian doctor who removed a child's tonsils for free when the parents couldn't afford it. Like so many others in the Kiwanis group, in addition to being generous with his time, Grosberg was also generous with monetary donations and donations of food for the various events the club sponsored.

Over the years he was a Kiwanian, Grosberg served on numerous committees, both on the local and state level. He was on the local Board of Directors and served as vice president in 1937 and 1938. In 1940 he served as president of the Schenectady club, a position he treasured.

Publicity photo of Joe Grosberg used when he was president of the Kiwanis Club. In the photo he is wearing his Kiwanis pin on his lapel.
Bellin Family Archives

Two other positions Grosberg was proud to hold were head of the camp committee which allowed underprivileged children to attend summer camp, and chairman of the Kiwanis boys and girls committee.

As a Kiwanian, Grosberg would have the fun of dressing in event-appropriate attire such as a chef's hat and apron for a cookout. During one fund raiser, he and another member staged a fist fight on the corner of State Street and Erie Blvd, pretending to fight over the rights to sell newspapers on that spot for Kids' Day. When a crowd formed to watch the mock fight, newspapers were sold to help raise funds.[25]

In Everett S. Lee's The Story of The Kiwanis Club of Schenectady, Lee wrote about a Kiwanis prank that Grosberg recalled from when Franklin Roosevelt was governor of New York in the late 1920s or early 1930s.

> On one occasion, Charlie Eldridge, Joe Grosberg, and Everett Lee were driving to an Inter-Club Meeting at Warrensburg. Joe, one of our

Charter Members was beaming as he was recalling some of the Kiwanis pranks of old. Someone said, "Tell us about the kidnapping of New York State Governor Franklin Delano Roosevelt." Joe beamed some more and complied:

> The Kiwanis Club of Schenectady and the Kiwanis Club of Amsterdam had arranged an Inter-Club Meeting at which Governor Roosevelt was to be the speaker. The meeting was to be in the Amsterdam Armory, and arrangements were made that the Governor's car could be driven right to the head table. At the meeting time, there was no Franklin, so we waited and waited.
>
> After waiting an hour, Franklin finally came. He had been stopped enroute by what he assumed was a welcoming committee from our Clubs, but it was a group from another Kiwanis Club, who kidnapped him for their meeting, then sent him on to us. Did you say fun? We had it.[26]

As the years went by, the original 90 members of the Schenectady Kiwanis Club dropped out or died off. For the rest of his life, Grosberg continued to be honored by the group as a charter member. Prior to his death in 1971, he had the distinction of being the last surviving charter member of the Schenectady Kiwanians. His membership in the club lasted over 52 years.

Grosberg was also a member of the Elks Club for more than 25 years, as well as a 32nd degree Mason (Cyprus Temple in Albany) and a member of the Zion Lodge 909, Independent Order of Odd Fellows (I.O.O.F.).

Joe Grosberg, wearing his Shriners/Freemason's Fez.
Bellin Family Archives

Other Community Involvement

During the first World War, Grosberg showed his patriotism in many ways, including offering his services and money to The Schenectady Home Defense League. He was part of a sub-committee that reported on the food stocks of the city every week so that if supplies fell below a critical point, action could be taken to conserve the supply or arrange for substitutes.

During WWII, Schenectady War Council Chairman and Director of the Emergency Welfare Services Leo H. Vosburg contacted Grosberg to determine the advisability of purchasing food stock for the emergency welfare centers if a bomb was ever dropped on the Schenectady area. Grosberg told him, "In the event of any disaster my complete warehouse stocks will be at your disposal, and if there is any item we don't have, we'll get it for you." According to Vosburg, it was deemed, "as fine a patriotic gesture as any made, for it eliminated the problem of stocking and storing large quantities of food by the welfare centers, something other communities at the time were worrying about."[27]

As a member of The Merchants Association of Schenectady Grosberg helped promote the sale of Liberty Bonds by advertising the bonds in store windows and encouraging employees to buy what they could afford. He was a member of the Schenectady Business Men's Association and served on the executive committee of the Second Ward Taxpayers' Association in Schenectady.

In 1925, Grosberg led the effort of organizing a committee to create The Schenectady Traffic Improvement Association to help improve traffic flow around Schenectady. Around this time, Schenectady merchants were frustrated with the lack of traffic lights and proper traffic flow around the city which often caused difficulties for their truck drivers in making deliveries in a timely manner. Grosberg was initially named temporary chairman of the committee to get the association started.[28] Later, he was officially named chairman of the association.

Grosberg was active in many fund drives including the Schenectady Chamber of Commerce Community Chest to benefit welfare/community agencies and Schenectady War Chest to benefit war organizations or purposes directly or indirectly related to the war. From 1925 through at least 1948, Grosberg served on many Community Chest and War Chest committees, and at times, served as director or committee head and/or board member. Grosberg practiced what he preached while helping to raise funds, and contributed much of his own money to the cause.

In 1930 Grosberg was part of a special committee appointed by the chairman of the mayor's finance committee to determine how to raise money to care for families and individuals needing assistance because of unemployment during the Great Depression. All money donated would be used exclusively for unemployment relief.

In 1944, Grosberg was on a public relations committee for the USO, a military support organization that aided military service members and their families. In 1944, Grosberg also volunteered to be on a panel for the Schenectady War Price and Rationing Board to help check prices in grocery stores to determine compliance with price ceilings.

Grosberg was a supporter of St Clare's Hospital. Plans for building a Catholic hospital in the Schenectady area were in the works for many years, but at times stalled due to WWII and other issues. Grosberg, a practicing Jew, did not let the Catholic part get in the way of helping out. He saw a need for the hospital and rose to the occasion. When a dinner meeting of 300 businessmen and civic leaders was held at the Van Curler Hotel in June of 1945 to outline plans for the new Catholic hospital, Grosberg was one of a handful of men to host the dinner. Grosberg served on the citizens executive committee to help raise money to build St Clare's Hospital. At the opening ceremony for the new hospital, Grosberg was one of the founders seated on the dais.

Grosberg was also one of the founders of the Troy (Capital District) Jewish Home for the Aged, which was later called Daughters of Sarah Jewish Home for the Aged. Some of the early planning for the Jewish elderly home got started in the Grosbergs' living room. Over the years, Grosberg held a number of different roles and titles for the home, including serving on the board of directors and board of trustees for many years, as late as 1968. He was chairman of the Executive Committee, and chairman of the Schenectady fund drive in 1947. In 1950 he was one of the vice presidents, and in 1954 was honorary vice president.

In 1952, Grosberg was appointed general chairman of the Schenectady Civil Defense food supply section. In July 1954, he was appointed by the county Civil Defense Director the position of chairman of the committee. The committee consisted of prominent food dealers who would administer food supply for the county civil defense supply section.

Grosberg was on the Board of Directors of Saratoga Springs Cure and Convalescent Home starting in 1931. The Saratoga Springs Cure and Convalescent Home was an institution of hydrotherapy, and provided room, board, and Sulphur and mud baths. It was a combination spa and convalescent home, providing free care for those who couldn't afford it. The home's original name was the Judea Convalescent Home, but switched to the new name in order to stress that the "health camp" was available to non-Jews as well as Jewish patients. The home was located on Jefferson Street in

Saratoga Springs, NY. It originally was opened only during the summer months, but later went year round.

Grosberg's energy and devotion to the causes he believed in was endless. Being a natural leader, he was often appointed or nominated to head newly-established groups. Many times, he volunteered when no one else was willing to do a job. He was often invited to speak in front of groups, sometimes as the guest speaker, sometimes to open a meeting, and sometimes as master of ceremonies. He often served as a judge for youth contests or events in the area. He was always attending dinners, meetings, openings, and conventions. He represented the Schenectady Jewish community at large, and he represented business leaders, most especially the grocery and supermarket industry.

The activities mentioned here are just some examples of Grosberg's involvement with professional organizations, community groups, and charitable causes. It's hard to believe with everything he was involved in, he had any spare time left, but he still found time to play an occasional round of golf. In 1929 when the new Shaker Ridge Country Club in Albany County opened, Grosberg was one of the original members. Being a member of the country club wasn't all play and no work for him--he also served on the Shaker Ridge Board of Governors. He remained a member of the country club for many decades, possibly until the end of his life.

Real Estate Holdings

During his lifetime, Grosberg purchased a good deal of real estate around Schenectady. Often property he purchased was put in his wife's name, most likely for asset protection in the event someone tried to sue him or one of his businesses. Records have been located for several dozen real estate purchases the Grosbergs made during their lives. Below are just some of them he was involved in, as well as some early real estate transactions involving his parents. This list is not complete, and does not include any of the real estate purchased under Grosberg's company, Central Markets, Inc. Dates listed are approximate. Some of the information regarding these properties were found within newspaper listings, thus the details regarding them might not be completely accurate. Land records could not be located to validate the earliest Grosberg holdings.

1911: Parents Jacob and Anna Grosberg sold or transferred ownership of *Lot 25, Hattie Place* in Schenectady to their son, Joe.[29]

1913: (August) Joe and Rae sold part of Lot 25, *Hattie Street* (formerly Hattie Place).[30]

1914: (Oct. 5): Jacob and Son purchased *Glenville Lot 51* map Crestline Park.[31] They owned this vacant lot at least through December 1921 when it appeared on a list for unpaid taxes.

1915: The Grosbergs' store, Jacob and Son, was located at *448 South Centre (Center) Street**, and the family also lived in the same building. Jacob Grosberg was listed as the owner in 1909, but the property was in Anna Grosberg's name when it was sold or transferred to Joe in 1915.

***Note**: The South Centre Street address in Schenectady where the Grosbergs once lived no longer exists and the building they owned is no longer there. Before 1900, a section of Broadway from State Street to Weaver Street was known as South Centre (or Center) Street. Later, South Centre became part of Broadway. It is believed that their 448 South Centre address became 148 Broadway, placing the location between Hamilton Avenue and State Street.*

1915: Jacob and Anna Grosberg sold or transferred a lot on *Crane Street* as well as a lot on *Van Guysling Avenue* to Joe.[32] Most likely, the Van Guysling property was *47 Van Guysling*. That was the address of Jacob and Son prior to 1915, then by 1916, the same building was used for Joseph E. Grosberg Wholesale Grocery Store. The brick building was three stories high, plus a basement, and had a garage, stables, and sheds on the property. The building included office and warehouse space and was equipped with an electric freight elevator and steam heat. In 1916 a fire broke out and gutted the three-story building. Grosberg rebuilt and repaired the damage from the fire. When Grosberg moved his business to Erie Blvd, he leased the Van Guysling building to Lewis Golub starting in 1926. While Golub was leasing it, another fire broke out in 1927 at that same warehouse building. The fire was confined to a two-story frame addition behind the main three-story brick building. Lewis Golub and his sons continued doing business at the Van Guysling warehouse through 1930, up until the time that they merged their business with Grosberg's.

The front of the warehouse on Van Guysling when the Golubs rented it from Joe Grosberg from around 1926 until they became business partners in 1930. The "to let" sign posted on the building has "Jos. Grosberg" as the contact person. *Photo courtesy of Schenectady County Historical Society*

In December 1935 a property transfer listing in the Schenectady Gazette stated that the property located at *47-49 Van Guysling Avenue* owned by Rae Grosberg (not Joe) was transferred to Samuel Garbowitz who used it as a waste material warehouse.[33]

In 1937 history repeated itself again when yet another fire broke out in the building now owned by Garbowitz.

Another property transfer listing in the Schenectady Gazette on October 4, 1948 stated that *47 Van Guysling Avenue* was transferred from Rae Grosberg to Edward and Nathan Cohen. Although the building number is the same as that which Samuel Garbowitz purchased 11 years earlier, it's possible the land around it was divided up and sold to multiple buyers.

1920-1923 (approximate): *5-7 Schuyler Street, Amsterdam* – It is unknown if Grosberg Grocery Co., Inc. owned this store, or leased it. This is the building where Grosberg's Amsterdam wholesale business was first located. A notice in the May 3-4, 1920 Amsterdam Evening Recorder read, "Joseph E. Grosberg, Wholesale Grocer, is now located at 5 and 7 Schuyler Street. Telephone 1564."

1925-1932 (approximate): *152-160 West Main Street, Amsterdam*. After conducting business on Schuyler Street, Grosberg Grocery moved to 152-160 West Main Street. The building was owned under the business name Grosberg Grocery Co., Inc. Instances of business being conducted at this address have been found as late as 1932, but a September 27, 1927 real estate transfer notice said property on West Main Street, Amsterdam was transferred from Grosberg Grocery Company to John G. Doak and wife, so the property near 152 West Main Street owned by the company may have been subdivided. S. & G. Cramer, Inc. who Grosberg sold his shares of the Grosberg Grocery Company to continued doing business from this address as late as 1938, possibly later.

1927 through 1940s: *The Imperial Building* on the corner of State and Broadway in downtown Schenectady was one of the better-known buildings that Grosberg co-owned. The Imperial Building was always credited as being owned by Abe Cohen, a good friend of Grosberg's. While Cohen owned the popular Imperial clothing store that was located in the building and he was often referred to as the owner of the building, both he and Grosberg were co-owners of the building starting in May 1927.

Right after purchasing the building, Grosberg and Cohen invested an additional $125,000 to remodel the three-story brick structure into an up-to-date store and office building with terra-cotta front.[34] There were to be 9 stores housed in the building. The renovations were supposed to be completed by August of 1927, but the final remodel ended up being completed closer to October of that year. In October, a full-page ad ran in the Schenectady Gazette featuring ads of contractors and supplies who worked on the remodel.

State Street Building with Cohen and Grosberg names as contacts to lease space.
Photo courtesy of Schenectady County Historical Society

In 1932 Grosberg and Cohen petitioned against the city the assessment value of the Stanford property at State and Center (later called Broadway) asking for a reduction in assessment from $288,500 to $200,000.[35] Although property records of the building have not been found, newspaper articles from the time period suggest that Grosberg was co-owner of the Imperial Building at least through 1946.

Oct. 1930: Grosberg and Mayer Cramer together purchased *1000, 1002, & 1004 State Street* in Schenectady. Cramer was president of Mohawk Gas & Oil Corporation in Schenectady. He was also distantly related to Joe through marriage. Cramer was married to Rae Grosberg's cousin during his first marriage. After the death of his first wife, Cramer married a second time to Rae's niece.

In April 1931, Grosberg requested a building permit for a brick gas station on State and Swan Street, believed to be 1000 State Street.[36] In June of 1937, Grosberg transferred ownership of 1000, 1002 & 10004 State Street to Mayer Cramer.[37]

1920s-1960s: Grosberg purchased land and buildings all along *Erie Blvd*. Although not known for sure, it's possible he purchased a large piece of property on Erie and then subdivided it, or his Erie Blvd properties might have been different parcels of land that he bought up before and after the Erie Canal was filled in to become Erie Blvd in 1925. Following are some of the different Erie Blvd addresses that have been found for Grosberg.

1923-1940s (approximate): *271-273 Erie Blvd* Warehouse where Grosberg conducted his wholesale business, Joseph E. Gosberg, Inc. after moving from Van Guysling. This was the original offices and warehouse of Grosberg-Golub when the merger between the two wholesalers happened in 1930. In June or July of 1930, the property was transferred from Joseph E. Grosberg, Inc. to Joe Grosberg and his wife Rae, most likely to keep it a separate asset from the newly merged Grosberg-Golub company.

1929 (approximate): *110 Erie Blvd*. obtained a building permit for alteration of a garage in 1929.

1930s-1940s (approximate): *130 Erie Blvd*. This may have been a vacant parcel of land that Grosberg purchased and built on to expand his business. Grosberg and Golub, Inc. did business at this address, but Grosberg may have subdivided the land and sold or leased parts of it to other companies as many other companies were listed at that same address over the years. It's possible Grosberg may have owned the land as early as 1922, but this has not been confirmed.

1924-early 1960s (approximate): *140-142 Erie Blvd*. Grosberg purchased the C.S. Smith and Company Wholesale Grocers building, located near or next door to his wholesale warehouse building on Erie Blvd. While he continued to use the warehouse for his wholesale goods, he used the C.S. Smith building for office space for himself as well as leased out parts of the building to other businesses. He renamed the newly-purchased building the Grosberg Building. The building was located right down the street from G.E.'s headquarters. In 1925 Grosberg was approached by Mrs. Joseph (Mary) MacDonald for a lease for an all-night diner in the building. Grosberg agreed to make accommodations to the Grosberg Building for the diner. A portion of the first floor of the building was cut out and a corner of the building was removed to allow the 40-foot restaurant on wheels to nestle inside the building structure. Once the Grosberg Building had been modified, the diner was pulled up the boulevard, then backed it into the building where it remained for nearly 40 years.[38]

The municipal assessed value of the building in 1930 was $140,000, but Grosberg and his wife petitioned that it was valued at no more than $100,000. In 1932 they asked for another reduction from $130,00 to $90,000. This was in spite of an agreement reached the previous year between the city and the owners of the building that the owners would not start any certiorari action (petitioning the court for review) the next year.

In 1930, renovations to the front of the building were made, including installing a large "Grosberg Building" sign at the top of the building. Around November of 1930, Grosberg leased the upstairs floor of the Grosberg Building to Harry Teets, a former national roller-skating champion. After some modifications, Teets opened up Palace Roller Rink in January of 1931. When it opened, the rink was touted as one of the largest in that part of New York State. Initially, a 3,000-pound, one-of-a-kind Rudolph Wurlitzer band organ was installed to provide music for the skaters. Later, an organist playing a Hammond organ provided the music for skaters. Skating sessions were held afternoons and evenings. The Palace Roller Rink continued to operate in the building through 1949, and possibly beyond. A ballroom called the Silver Slipper leased space in the building around 1931/1932 and Barron-Burtiss Used Cars rented space starting around 1931, doing business there for several years. National Auto resided in the building for many years.

Building on Erie Blvd, with enlargement of the "Grosberg Building" sign on top.
Photo courtesy of Schenectady County Historical Society

When Grosberg retired as president of the Grosberg-Golub, Inc. in 1943, he kept ownership of 140 Erie Blvd. His former business partners, Ben and William Golub, continued to lease office space from him for their newly-renamed Golub Corporation. The Golubs stayed in the Grosberg building until the early 1960s. General Electric also leased offices in the building.

The space where the diner that was built into the Grosberg building continued to be leased by Mrs. MacDonald until around 1953, when she sold the diner to Mr. and Mrs. Thomas Hayner and they took over the lease. Last known as Hayner's Diner, the diner was removed from the Grosberg Building in September 1964, after Grosberg finally sold the building.

In January 1963, Grosberg sold the Grosberg building on Erie Blvd to Carl Liss for his business, the Carl Liss Appliance Company.

1948 (or earlier)-1954: Another landmark building Grosberg co-owned for a period of time was the G.E. Emmons' house at *1227 Wendell Avenue*. The 17-room estate bordered the Union College grounds and was originally the home of General Electric executive G.E. Emmons. The 3-story house featured 9 bedrooms, a lounge, a library, and a butler's pantry, among other amenities. The Emmons' house was purchased by Maude M. Killeen in April 1934 and stood vacant for 12 years prior to Grosberg and Samuel Scheinzeit purchasing it from Killeen on September 13, 1946 for $12,000[39]. Samuel Scheinzeit was the owner of the popular Apex Department Store and a personal friend of Grosberg's. The two men invested about $7,000 on renovations to the Emmons' house. In March of 1948, the two owners entered into a contract to sell the house to the fraternal organization Delta Chi of Union College for $25,000, contingent on the term that the organization was able to get zoning modifications in the single family neighborhood that would allow them to use the house as a fraternity residence.

After twice failing to get the zoning modification they requested, on April 5, 1948 the fraternal organization went ahead and had Delta Chi members move into the house anyway. The move-in turned up the heat on the zoning battle with the City. Residents of the neighborhood pitted against the Alumni Association of Union Chapter,

Neighbors and the City claimed the house was in a single-family residential zone and should not be used as housing for multiple, unrelated occupants. Lawyers for the fraternal organization tried to argue that members of the organization were a family, so fell under the single-family category. At first the battle was only against the City and the fraternal organization, but in May of 1948, Grosberg and Scheinzeilt, were brought into the proceedings as co-defendants on the technicality that they were still the owners of the property under the conditional terms of the pending sale.

The zoning and subsequent court battle dragged on for years with the fraternity continuing to occupy the house without a resolution being made. Grosberg and Scheinzeilt remained owners of the property since the pending sale had not yet been completed. The fraternity leased the house from Grosberg and Scheinzeilt while the court case continued.

In July 1954, the fraternity finally took ownership of the house from Grosberg and Scheinzeilt, and the two men were released from the on-going lawsuit. City residents continued to fight the fraternal organization's occupancy in the house for 11 years. The case was brought to the State Supreme Court and the residents won against the fraternal organization for violating zoning restrictions. Even after the win, fraternity members continued to reside in the house as "illegal residents" of the single-family neighborhood, while they appealed the verdict. In October of 1956 the fraternal organization sold the house to the First Unitarian Society of Schenectady with the understanding that Delta Chi members could continue to live in the house until June 1959. After Delta Chi vacated the house, it was torn down to make way for a new church.

Vintage post card circa early 1900s showing the G. E. Emmons house which eventually became the Delta Chi house and sparked a long-term court battle.

1952-1956: In September 1952, Grosberg purchased a garage and office building known at the time as the *Fuller Street Car Barn* from the bankrupt Schenectady

Railway Company at auction for $210,000. The car barn was where Schenectady Railway used to house their trolleys, then later buses. Grosberg's purchase of the car barn was the biggest individual sale at the Schenectady Railway bankruptcy auction. Within a couple of weeks of purchasing the property, Grosberg leased the building to the owners of the Troy-Schenectady Bus Company to use as a bus garage. He and the bus company tried, without success, to get the garage to become a major bus terminal, offering to finance all the renovations to turn the building into a bus depot in exchange for requiring the four separate bus lines operating under city permits to use the depot.

One of the legalities that plagued the Fuller Street property from the start was that the city claimed the building Grosberg purchased encroached on 10 feet of city property along the Erie Blvd side. Because of this, the city hit Grosberg up with penalty fees and until they were paid, Grosberg could not get a clear title to the property. Meetings and negotiations for the bus terminal continued, and one of the conditions Grosberg requested was waiving the penalty fees.[40] During the time all sides fought for or against the bus depot, the encroachment penalty fees added up to more than $30,000. The bus depot idea was finally vetoed. A few years later in May of 1956, Grosberg sold the property and buildings at a loss to Electric Union Hall, Inc.

Sidenote: At the same bankruptcy auction where Grosberg purchased the Fuller Street Garage, Central Markets, Inc. which had a store nearby purchased Schenectady Railway's McCellan Street garage along with five acres of land for $150,000. They planned to use part of the land for a parking lot. Grosberg was already out of Central Markets at that point and was not part of that deal.[41]

1944-1957: Grosberg Building at the Jewish Community Center, <u>*Germania Ave*</u>, Schenectady. Although technically owned by Joe and Rae Grosberg, the Schenectady Jewish Community Center had free use of the building. In November of 1957, Grosberg signed over the deed to the JCC and papers were filed in April 1958 giving them full ownership of the building.

Grosberg Family Members

The Grosberg Family, circa 1920s.
Front Row: Joseph, Jacob, Anna, and Charles.
Back Row: Harold, Marion, Benjamin, Ruth, William, and Myer.
Photo courtesy of Aaron Soifer

Parents

Jacob Grosberg was a quiet man and deeply religious. The year he was born varies in naturalization forms, census documents, and death certificates as being either 1858, 1861 or 1863, but his headstone lists his birth year as 1861. It is believed Jacob's first name (in Hebrew) was Yaakov and his original surname was Gans[42]. He was the son of Joseph and Miriam Gans. Although it's likely he had little formal education, he was a very learned man when it came to Judaism teachings, laws, and customs. He spent much of his free time studying the Torah and passed on his knowledge by teaching Hebrew school. His sons all treated him with great respect.

An early newspaper account in the *Troy Daily Times* from 1893 cited that there were warrants for the arrests of three men wanted for stealing wine from "Jacob Grosberg's place on River Street."[43] There is no proof this was actually the correct Jacob

Grosberg, but if it was, it means he probably owned a store prior to moving his family to Schenectady.

When Jacob and his family left Schenectady and moved to Detroit around 1915-1916, he planned to retire from the wholesale grocery business. His retirement, however, was short lived, and he ended up back in the wholesale grocery business in Detroit with his sons--officially with his fourth-born son, William, but Harry and Ben also worked with them. Their wholesale grocery store, J. Grosberg & Son, was initially located at 445 Russell Street in Detroit, but it is believed they moved their store to 249 Napolean Street sometime around 1917.

Jacob was married to Anna for 51 years before she passed away. After his wife's death in 1934, daughter Marion played matchmaker and fixed her father up with her widowed mother-in-law, Riza Schwarz. Jacob and Riza (sometimes spelled Risa) married in 1935 and spent six years together until Riza passed away in 1941. Jacob died in 1947 and was buried beside his first wife.

Jacob and Anna Grosberg, date unknown. *Bellin Family Archives*

Hannah (Anna) Lasky Grosberg was the daughter of Baruch and Rebecka Lasky. She came from Suwalki in Poland[44]. She was described by relatives as outspoken, warm-hearted and a generous soul. An example of her generosity was the time she walked into Synagogue wearing a coat, and left without it after giving it to someone who needed one more than she did. Her children's births were spread over a 20-year period, so their care, as well as taking care of her home, her husband, and assorted grandchildren was the focus of her life.

Anna suffered a fatal heart attack in 1934 in Detroit, Michigan at the age of 68. She was buried next to her son, Myer, who predeceased her in 1923.

Jacob and Anna Grosberg, July 1933. *Bellin Family Archives*

Siblings

Joe had five brothers and two sisters.

- Charles (1885-1968)
- Myer (1888-1929)
- William (three different birth years have been found: 1893/1894/1895-1978)
- Benjamin (1896-1987)
- Harold (1898-1972)
- Marion (1902-1997)
- Ruth (1903-1990)

The six Grosberg brothers, circa 1920s.
Front Row: Myer, Harold, and Ben
Back Row: Joseph, William, and Charles.
Photo courtesy of Margot Champagne

Charles (Charlie) Grosberg was Hannah (Anna) and Jacob Grosberg's second-born child after Joseph. There are conflicting records of where Charles was born. A 1900 census form lists that he was born in 1885 in Poland, the 1905 census says he was born in Russia, and a 1940 census says he was born in 1886 in New York. Most evidence point to him being born in Russia-Poland and came to the US when he was only a few months old.

Charles went into the wholesale grocery business in Detroit and his career followed a similar path as his brother Joseph's. Like Joe, Charles was considered a pioneer in the supermarket industry. Like Joe had done in the Schenectady area, Charles pioneered the wholesale "cash and carry" concept in Detroit. Also like his brother, Charles helped establish a group of independent merchants to band together in order to give them purchasing power.

Charles partnered up with John A. Reuter. Their firm, Grosberg & Reuter Wholesale Grocers, established a small chain of neighborhood retail grocery and meat markets. Charles' father-in-law, Joseph Wolf, was a retail grocer and Grosberg & Reuter merged their business with his. From 1915 through 1930 they operated under the trade name Wolf's Cash Markets. In 1931 they purchased Canners Warehouse, a company that was starting a downward slide after enjoying initial success. The company was renamed Packers Outlet, then later Packers Supermarket. The chain expanded to 41 units by the time Grosberg & Reuter sold it to the operators of the Wrigley Stores in 1951.

Over the years that Charles and Joe both worked in wholesale groceries and supermarkets, they enjoyed playfully competing against each other to see which brother's business was doing better. Charles' success eventually superseded his elder brother's.

Charles retired from the grocery business in the early 1950s and like his brother, spent his retirement years on philanthropy efforts, something else he and Joe liked to playfully compete at. Charles and his first wife Sadie (Wolf) had three children, Merwin (who celebrated his 105th birthday in 2017), Jeanne, and Norma. Sadie died in 1934 at the age of 46, just one month before Charles' mother passed away. Charles' second wife was Rose Davidsson.

Charles Grosberg, 1921. *Bellin Family Archives*

To read an article about Charles written by his son Merwin, check out: https://www.michjewishhistory.org/assets/docs/Journals/Michigan_Jewish_History_1985_01.pdf

Myer Grosberg was the third-born Grosberg son. He was more interested in academics than going into the family grocery business. He attended Yale University Medical School, class of 1912, studied science, but left college at the end of his junior year. He worked in Detroit for a short time before going back to school in Schenectady. He went on to graduate in 1915 with a B.S. degree from Union College. The following September he took a position at Yale University as a chemistry instructor, and at some point got his master's degree in chemistry. He moved back to Detroit, and worked in real estate sales. The spelling of his first name varies from source to source. His 1912 Yale yearbook spells his name Myer and lists his nickname as Mike. His 1917 draft card says Myer, but he signed it Max. Most census records have him down as Myer, but his cemetery headstone reads Meyer. In 1917 at the age of 29, he married Mary Brockow of Brooklyn, NY, but the marriage didn't last long. He ended up working in California, and wrote fiction under a pen name in his spare time. He passed away in 1923. He had no children.

Myer Grosberg, circa 1921. *Bellin Family Archives*

William (Billy/Bill) Grosberg was also a business man like his two oldest brothers. He and his father started a wholesale business together in Detroit called J. Grosberg and Son. He frequently went back and forth to Schenectady from Detroit and ended up marrying a Schenectady girl, Rose Morris, in June 1918. The two lived in Detroit for a while after they married.

In January 1925, William's brother-in-law, Harry Morris, died after falling three stories down an elevator shaft at the Schenectady company owned by his father and himself. William and Rose returned to Schenectady so that William could help his father-in-law with the business. In March 1926 William became one of the principal stock holders of S. Morris & Son, along with his father- and mother-in-law, Solomon and Dora Morris. In August of that same year, William invested a great deal of his savings in a dance hall called Blossom Heath on the Albany-Schenectady Road. He went to an insurance broker for insurance, but the broker had difficulty finding an insurance company willing to insure the building. The broker eventually went with several out-of-state insurance companies without obtaining the proper licensing required. Unfortunately, the broker started hearing rumors about the primary insurer, and so he wrote to them to cancel the insurance on the dance hall in August of 1928. About a week after the letter was sent, the dance hall burned down. Other than a couple of small insurance policies, the hall was largely uninsured. This caused the broker to lose his insurance license for a short period of time and sparked a lawsuit against him by William, who was nearly wiped out by the huge loss. In 1930, about two years after the dance hall fire, William and Rose returned to Detroit to live. After WWII they relocated to California. They had two children, Sanford and Phyllis.

William Grosberg, 1931. *Bellin Family Archives*

Benjamin (Ben/Bennie) Grosberg attended Yale University and was also involved in the grocery business for a while. In 1917 he worked as a store clerk in his father's and William's store, J. Grosberg and Son in Detroit, then later worked in his brother Charles' grocery business. A 1937 reference in "The Super Market; A Revolution In Distribution" by Max Mandell Zimmerman noted that Benjamin attended the first convention of the Super Market Institute and listed him as vice president of Packer's Outlets, the company owned by his brother Charles. Ben's first marriage was to Hattie Rabinowitz, and his second marriage was to Hattie's sister, Lee.

In the late 1950s, Benjamin co-owned a ten-horse stable at Yonkers Raceway, but in 1959 he had his owner license revoked by the New York State Harness Racing Commission. An investigation determined he made false statements on his application for an owner's license in 1955 when he failed to mention that he knowingly associated with persons associated with a bookmaker or a gambling establishment. His brother-in-law, Morris Robinson who was half-owner of the stables, admitted to being friendly with Philip Wall who had a record of 33 arrests and convictions from 1928 to 1957 for bookmaking. During the investigation, it was discovered that card games were held at the stables in which one of the ranking horse drivers and possibly other drivers played card games at the stables with the bookmaker. Benjamin's brother-in-law was barred from any participation in harness racing and was not permitted to enter any New York City track even as a spectator after the investigation. Although Benjamin lost his owner license for the stable, he continued to own horses that raced. Benjamin had one son, Herbert Grosberg, who was an accountant. Herbert gained notoriety in the 1950s for being Jimmy Hoffa's accountant, and for testifying against Hoffa in hearings led by Robert Kennedy.

Benjamin Grosberg sitting in front of J. Grosberg & Son's wholesale store in Detroit, circa 1921. *Bellin Family Archives*

Harold (Harry) Grosberg was the youngest Grosberg boy. He was still living at home at the age of 29 and his mother was pressuring him to settle down and marry. The blond hair, blue eyed boy attracted many hoping-to-marry girls, but his heart ended up going to a Schenectady girl. It was on a visit to his brother Joe back in Schenectady when he ran into Dorothy Vinick, a sweet, pretty girl he knew back in high school. At the "ripe old age of 29," she too was hoping to find a man to marry, and the timing was right for both of them.

Harold and Dorothy settled down in Detroit, where Harold worked in the family business with his father and brothers at J. Grosberg and Son. Later, Harold was listed as a partner and owner of the Packer-Outlet Supermarket Corp of Detroit, which was owned by his brother Charles. Harold's second wife was Lillian Grass.

Harold Grosberg on left, and Benjamin Grosberg center. The man on the right is believed to be Samuel Cramer, who was one of Joseph Grosberg's business partners in Amsterdam, NY. They are standing in front of the "J. Grosberg & Son" store in Detroit, circa 1921. *Bellin Family Archives*

Marion Grosberg was born in 1902. After six boys in a row the family finally had a girl. Marion's oldest brother Joe was 19 years old when she was born, so there was a big age difference. Marion (not to be confused with Joe's daughter Marian with an "a") married Robert Schwarz who worked in the grocery business in the Detroit area. They had three children, Jeanne, Marvin, and Alvin Schwarz.

Marion Grosberg, date unknown. *Bellin Family Archives*

Ruth Grosberg was born a year after her sister Marion. She was 20 years younger than her brother Joe. When Joe's first daughter Mildred was born, Ruth was only 5 years old. Being close in ages, Ruth and her niece Mildred had a close relationship, even though Mildred lived in Schenectady and Ruth lived in Detroit. Ruth married Abraham Gurwin and had a son, Hanley.

Ruth Grosberg, 1920. *Bellin Family Archives*

Joseph's Wife

Rachel (Rae) Greenberg was born in Poland in 1883 to Moses (Morris) Kadisky and Rebecca (Bessie) Freida Greenberg. It was a second marriage for both Rae's parents. Her father was widowed with two children from his first wife, a daughter Hannale (Hannah) and a son whose name is unknown. Rae's mother Rebecca, who was called Bessie, was also widowed and had a daughter named Pearl from her first husband. After Moses/Morris and Rebecca/Bessie married, they had two more children together, Rachel (Rae) and a baby boy whose name is unknown.

In 1887 Bessie Greenberg Kadisky left Poland with young Rae for the United States to join Bessie's sister living in Troy, New York. Rae was told her father and baby brother had died of an illness in Poland. The 1910 US census form substantiates the story of Bessie having another child by stating that she had given birth to 3 children, but only 2 were living. Rae's half-sister Pearl from her mother's first marriage did not travel to the United States with Rae and Bessie. Pearl's paternal grandparents convinced Bessie to leave Pearl with them in Poland, claiming Pearl was the only thing they had left of their deceased son (Bessie's first husband). Pearl was about 4 years older than Rae, so she was probably about 7 years old at the time. She ended up staying in Poland until her adult years. Rae's half-brother and half-sister from her father's first marriage also didn't come to the United State right away. It is believed they were both over the age of 18 by the time Bessie and Rae left Poland, and they may have already been married with families of their own.

When Bessie arrived in the US, she and Rae took Bessie's maiden name of Greenberg as their last name, completely abandoning the surname of Kadisky. No one knows for certain why Bessie changed their last name, but according to family members she may not have wanted her second husband's family finding her.

In New York, Bessie and Rae Greenberg moved in with Bessie's sister Esther Jennie Greenblath (who went by the name Jennie) and brother-in-law Morris Greenblath. Morris and Jennie lived in a four-story brownstone on First Street in Troy and it was there Rae spent the rest of her childhood.

Rachel Greenberg, circa 1886-1887.
Bellin Family Archives

The Greenblaths eventually had six children. Rae was the oldest child living in the house, and she and her Greenblath cousins grew up like siblings. One cousin didn't even realize Rae wasn't her real sister until they were older and noticed they had slightly different last names—Greenberg instead of Greenblath.

Rae was a highly-intelligent girl. When she completed grade 8 with the highest marks in her class, the principal of the school called in her mother to discuss her future. He praised Rae's intelligence and recommended that if Bessie didn't need Rae to help at home or didn't need her to get a job to help support the family, Rae should be allowed to continue with her education by going on to high school. At that time, around 1896-1897, many girls didn't go on to high school. Bessie would have permitted her daughter to continue with her schooling if Rae wanted to, but Rae decided since none of the other girls in her class were going, she wouldn't either, so her formal education ended at 8th grade. Later in her life, Rae regretted that decision.[45]

Rachel Greenberg, age 14.
Bellin Family Archives

Joseph's Daughters

All three of Joe and Rae's daughters were remarkable, highly-intelligent girls. Luckily, they had a father who believed his daughters should get a higher education and could afford to pay for it--even during the Depression years. The Grosberg girls all received their undergraduate degrees from Smith College, with Mildred graduating in 1928, Rozzie in 1934, and Marian in 1936.

Mildred Grosberg (1908-2008) was the oldest of the three Grosberg girls. She graduated at the top of her class at Schenectady High School at the age of 15 and went on to graduate from Smith College in 1928. After college she took a position working in the office of the Albany Jewish Community Center (JCC). A couple of weeks into her job the staff doctor at the JCC, Dr. Harold Bellin, became smitten with her and asked her to lunch. The doctor asked her out to lunch again a second time, and the third time he asked her to lunch he also asked her to marry him. The two married in 1931.

Mildred was the author of a number of popular Jewish cookbooks that stayed in print for decades. In 1934 her first cookbook, *Modern Kosher Meals*, was published, and later was reissued as *Modern Jewish Meals*. Her best-known book was *The Jewish Cookbook*, published in 1941, updated in 1958, reissued in 1983 as *The Original Jewish Cookbook*, and in 2017, nine years after her death, was published once again in e-version. For several years, Mildred wrote a syndicated column about Jewish cooking, as well as articles for newspapers and magazines on Jewish cooking.

<u>Rosalind (Rozzie) Grosberg</u> (1912- 2003) was Joseph's and Rae's middle daughter. In 1926 at the age of 13 she was a champion speller who represented Schenectady County in the New York State Spelling Bee. She was a salutatorian of her high school class and graduated Phi Beta Kappa from Smith College in 1934. She married her husband, Mortimer (Morty) Cohen in 1936. When she was in her 40's she went back to school at Albany State Teacher's College and earned her teaching credential. She then worked teaching home-bound children.

<u>Marian Grosberg</u> (1915-1993) was Joe and Rae's youngest daughter. A Smith College graduate like her two older sisters before her, she also did post-graduate work at Columbia School of Journalism. Writing was Marian's passion. Throughout college and long after, she was always penning something, including ghost writing for political figures. In 1940, Marian married Mildred's husband's nephew, Herbert (Herbie) Champagne, the son of Harold Bellin's oldest sister, Mary Bellin Champagne.

Marian continued with her education at Albany Law School, and after receiving her law degree in 1955, she joined her husband working in his law office. Her first novel, "The Cauliflower Heart" was published in 1944. Her second novel, "Quimby & Son," published in 1962, was about a girl whose grandfather and father were in the wholesale grocery business.[46] Although fiction, it detailed a lot of what Marian and her sisters lived through growing up as daughters of a wholesale grocer. In the book, the main character Anita talks about "sliding down the hills of sugar sacks," the same way both Mildred and Rosalind in later interviews talked about playing on them. The fictitious Anita talked about "dirtying the long white stockings," and eating nuts out of drawers, and of her father trying to convince his father to move into the wholesale grocery business, all things that happened in the real Grosbergs' world. The book also detailed how the main character wanted to work in the business, but couldn't because women didn't go into business in those days. When Marian was in her 20s she worked for her father's company, writing slogans for Central Market's advertisements. It is believed Marian had a desire to be more involved in her father's grocery business when she was young, but like her lead character in "Quimby & Son," she didn't have the opportunity within the company that a son might have had available to him. Instead of going into the family business, Marian ended up with two other careers, one as a writer and the other an attorney.

Joe and Rae's daughters, Rosalind (front), Marian (back left), Mildred (back right). June 1934. *Bellin Family Archives*

Rae's Mother

Rebecca (Bessie) Freida Greenberg was a quiet woman, and extremely religious. She always wore a wig in the Orthodox Jewish tradition of married women never showing their hair in public. At one point, Bessie earned a living by loaning money to area immigrants who were not able to buy on credit, or needed money to pay off their debts. She then collected the money over time from those loans, along with interest. Her job involved a lot of walking, and she traveled all over the area to collect from the people who owed her money. Bessie could speak both English and Hebrew, and it is believed she also know how to read and write, which would have given her an advantage running a business for other immigrants. In a 1943 newspaper death notice for Bessie's brother-in-law Morris Greenblath, it stated he was a retired credit merchant, so Bessie may have learned about running a loan business from him.[47] Where a single widowed woman got the initial funds to start up her own loan business is unknown, but it may have been borrowed from her brother-in-law, or it may have been from saving her own money from an earlier job. On the 1910 US census form, Bessie's occupation was listed as "Retail Merchant, Dry Goods," the same occupation listed that year for Morris Greenblath.

With the money Bessie earned working or loaning money to immigrants, she supported herself and Rae, as well as sent money back to Poland for her daughter Pearl. She also paid room and board to her brother-in-law to live in his house, and contributed to the cooking and housework in the Greenblath home.

Bessie Greenberg, circa 1921. *Bellin Family Archives*

Bessie lived with her sister Jennie and brother-in-law Morris for nearly 50 years, from the time she arrived in the US in 1887 until the end of her life in 1936. After death, Bessie, Jennie, and Morris shared a family cemetery stone marked "Greenblath/ Greenberg" in Beth Tephilah Cemetery in Troy, New York.

Rae's Siblings

Rae's half-siblings from her father's side, *Hannah (Kadisky)* Engle and a brother (name unknown), came to the US at some point. Hannah, who was called Annie, ended up in Pennsylvania. She knew her stepmother Bessie and half-sister Rae were somewhere in the US, but didn't know where. She would ask every traveling salesman who passed through the area if he knew of a Jewish widow with a daughter around Rae's age. Eventually, one traveling salesman did say he knew of one who fit the description up in Troy, and going on that tip, Hannah was able to find them. Rae was thrilled to reconnect with her half-sister, and based on stories passed down, she might not have known she even had another sister until Hannah suddenly appeared on their doorstep. Her mother never talked about her life back in Poland and might not have told Rae about her second husband's children from his first marriage, or Rae may have been too young to remember them. Hannah and her children eventually moved from Pennsylvania to the Schenectady area, and her sons took jobs working for Joe. Nothing is known about the half-brother who came to the US, other than he may have at one time lived in the Boston, MA area.

Rae's other half-sister on her mother's side, *Pearl*, spent her whole childhood in Poland. She married a man with the last name Cooper (first name unknown), had three children, and at some point was widowed. It was sometime after World War I, around 1919-1920, that Joseph Grosberg along with relatives of Pearl's deceased husband, paid for the widowed Pearl and her children to come to the United States. Pearl and her children made their home in Brooklyn, NY, where her husband's relatives lived, but her sons, and possibly the rest of the family, ended up in the Schenectady area for a time.

Grosberg Family Photos

Bellin Family Archives

Bellin Family Archives

Miscellaneous Items of Interest

Names of Businesses

Over the years he worked in the grocery field Joseph Grosberg did business under various names. Some of these include the following:

1903-1920: *Jacob Grosberg and Son* - company Joseph and his father Jacob ran in Schenectady.

Starting in 1920: *Joseph E. Grosberg, Inc.* - Schenectady business incorporated under Joseph's own name after his father moved to Detroit.

Starting in 1920: *Grosberg Grocery Company, Inc*. - Amsterdam business incorporated with Samuel and George Cramer of Amsterdam.

Approximately 1922-1930: *Grosberg Packing Company* - Many references were found in newspapers of the company doing business under this name. It was also the company name Grosberg used to file a patent and trademark for Snow Baby canned vegetables, fruits, and spices.

1930: *Double GG Grocery Company, Inc.* - Name used briefly when Joseph E. Grosberg and Company, Inc. first merged with Golub's Cash and Carry.

Approximately 1931-1944: *Grosberg-Golub Company, Inc*. - Schenectady wholesale business name changed from the Double GG Company, Inc.

1933: *Grosberg-Cramer Grocery Company* - Amsterdam business name changed from the Grosberg Grocery Company.

May 23, 1933: Public Service Center, Inc. - The first two original Central Market stores first opened under this entity.

August 31, 1933: *Central Market, Inc.* - Grosberg-Golub Company incorporated Central Markets as a separate entity.

1935: *Super-Markets, Inc.* - Initial mention of this company in a newspaper article had Grosberg listed as heading this a new firm under this name and a principal "subscriber", and a second newspaper article mentions the new supermarket was opened under his personal direction, but no other record or report could be found of his involvement.

Central Markets Stores Opened During the Grosberg-Golub Years

According to newspaper articles announcing Grosberg's retirement in September of 1943, there were twelve Central Market stores and two department stores being operated by Grosberg- Golub, Inc. at that time. A June 1942 article claimed there were fourteen Central Market stores, which may have included the two department stores in that count. In researching, the author has found mention of fifteen Central Market stores (not including the two department stores) during the years Grosberg was involved in the company. Reasons for the discrepancy could be because some stores may have opened, then closed by the time Grosberg retired, or some stores may have moved to a new location so were counted as two different stores. The information below is a list of Central Market Stores opened prior to Grosberg's retirement, as best as the author could ascertain. They are listed in the order they were opened, if the opening date is known.

1. **November 1932** - *Paine and Swan Street, Green Island, Troy*. The first supermarket store opened by Grosberg-Golub was originally called *Public Service Market*, although many advertisements from 1933 and 1934 called it the *Public Service Economy Market* and at least one ad in 1933 called it the *Public Service Economy Center*.
2. **March 1933** - corner *Broadway and 14th /14th Street and 2nd Avenue* (circa 1934 *1600 Broadway) in Watervliet*. Watervliet Central Market, sometimes called *Watervliet Central Cash Market*.
3. **August 1933** - *1639 Eastern Parkway, Schenectady*. This was the first store called *Central Market*. When this store opened, they changed the two previous stores' names to *Central Market* as well.
4. **March 30, 1934** - *2600 Guilderland Ave, Schenectady*. This store was referred to as the Bellevue branch store to distinguish it from the first Schenectady store.
5. **December 21, 1934** - *30 Cooper Street, Glens Falls*.
6. **Pre-1935** - 6 102nd Street, Lansingburg, Troy.
7. **Pre-1937** - *431-433 Broadway, Saratoga Springs*.
8. **1936** - *389 First Street at Jackson Street, South Troy.*
9. **1937** - *29-31 South Main Street, Mechnicville*. One newspaper article said this was the 8th Central Market store, others said there were 9 stores when this one opened.
10. **May 1938** - *226-228 Broadway, Schenectady*. This was the third Schenectady Central Market.
11. **November 1938** - *331-339 Columbia in Utica*.
12. **Pre-December 1938** - *363-365 5th Ave at 109th Street, North Troy*.
13. **February 1941** - *325 Madison Avenue, Albany* corner of Madison and Swan. When first opened one newspaper article said it was the 12th store.

14. **Pre-1942** - *222 Broadway, Albany*.
15. **Pre-1944** - *66-68 South Pearl, Albany*.

Department Stores

1. **1940** - *DeFreest Department Store*, 103 Remaen Street, Cohoes, NY. The DeFreest store was later sold to Floyd J. Kessler who at one time managed the store for the Golubs.
2. **Date unknown** - *Clark Department Store* - Ballston Spa, NY.

Grosberg Family Ties to the Grocery Business

When Joe Grosberg and his father Jacob first started in the grocery business, it was a family operation with all the Grosberg children pitching in. After Joe's parents and siblings moved from Schenectady, Joe continued using relatives as employees. Whenever anyone with any kind of family ties needed a job, "Uncle Joe" was the one to go to. His wife Rae acted as secretary in the early years of Grosberg's Wholesale Company, and on paper, at least, was listed as secretary whenever her husband incorporated any of his businesses. The following is a list of some other employees with family ties to Grosberg:

<u>Morris Greenblath</u> - In 1920 when Grosberg incorporated his general grocery business under the name Joseph E. Grosberg, Inc., he and Rae were the principal stockholders with Rae's uncle, Morris Greenblath, listed as the only other stockholder. Greenblath was married to Rae's maternal aunt Jennie.

<u>Nathan Levine</u> - Nathan Levine was affiliated with Grosberg going back to 1917, and possibly earlier. He was working as a salesman for the Grosberg Wholesale Company when he started dating the company's bookkeeper, Mary Greenblath, Rae Grosberg's cousin. Mary and Nathan were married at the Grosberg's home on Hamilton Street in 1919. When Grosberg merged his company with Lewis Golub's, Levine became assistant treasurer of the Grosberg-Golub Company. He served as manager of the Central Market on Eastern Avenue in Schenectady for about 16 years, and later was a regional supervisor for the company. After retirement, he continued a long friendship with Grosberg and his wife.

<u>Mary Greenblath</u> - Mary Greenblath was Rae Grosberg's cousin, daughter of Morris and Jennie Greenblath. For a time, Mary worked as a bookkeeper for the Grosberg Wholesale Company prior to marrying Nathan Levine.

<u>Samuel and George Cramer</u> - Brothers Sam and George were Grosberg's partners in the Grosberg Grocery Amsterdam business. Although technically not related to

Grosberg, their brother, Mayer was related to Grosberg by marriage (both Mayer's first and second wives were Rae's relatives).

Mayer Cramer - Mayer L. Cramer was married to Rae Grosberg's cousin, Anna (Annie) Greenblath. Rae was very close to Annie, and after Annie passed away from influenza in 1918, Rae stayed close to Mayer Cramer and his young daughter. Rae introduced Cramer to her niece, Ida Engle, daughter of her half-sister Hannah. The widower Cramer ended up marrying Ida, staying related to the Grosbergs by marriage the second time around as well. Mayer Cramer was president of Mohawk Gas & Oil Corporation in Schenectady. Although he wasn't involved with the grocery business with Grosberg like his brothers Sam and George Cramer were, he and Grosberg were involved in many of the same organizations, and the two at one point became real estate partners. In October 1930, Mayer and Joe purchased 1000, 1002, & 1004 State Street in Schenectady. They remained real estate partners for at least 7 years before Grosberg transferred ownership of the State Street properties over to Mayer.

Morris and Hyman Cooper - Joe Grosberg hired Rae Grosberg's half-sister Pearl's two sons, Morris and Hyman Cooper, to work for him when they moved to the Schenectady area. Hyman at one time was the director of the dry goods and cosmetics division of Central Markets (1941-1943 timeframe). In 1945, Hyman and Grosberg purchased a department store together in Burlington, VT.

Charles and Samuel Engle – sons of Rae Grosberg's half-sister Hannah, worked for a time for Grosberg, but it is unknown in what capacity.

Mortimer Cohen - Grosberg's son-in-law Mortimer (Morty) Cohen served in several different roles within Central Markets. He was Retail Grocery Supervisor for Central Markets for ten years. He also served as manager of the Madison Avenue Central Market store in Albany around 1941, and was listed as a spokesman for the Central Market employees at Grosberg's retirement dinner. One newspaper article indicated at one point Cohen was vice president of Frank's Economy Store in Burlington, Vermont, a department store purchased by Grosberg and his wife's nephew, but little else could be found to verify that role. Cohen was married to the Grosberg's middle daughter, Rosalind.

Marian Grosberg - Grosberg's youngest daughter Marian did some advertising work for Central Markets, writing slogans and jingles for the company.

Lila Bellin - Grosberg's daughter Mildred's sister-in-law, Lila Bellin, was hired as a sign painter for Central Markets.

Advertisements

Below are samplings of some advertisements from Grosberg's businesses.

Early ads listing Jacob Grosberg and Son on South Center (Centre) as distributors for Duluth Imperial Flour. Various Duluth ads with different recipes were run continuously in the Schenectady Gazette throughout 1912.

Schenectady Gazette, Nov. 12, 1912, p.6. (*fultonhistory.com*)

Schenectady Gazette, Aug. 6, 1912, p.5. (*fultonhistory.com*)

U.S. Grain Corporation Ad, January 29, 1920, Schenectady Gazette. (*fultonhistory.com*)

Coffee Ad, 1928, Amsterdam Recorder. (*fultonhistory.com*)

Budweiser Malt Syrup Ad, June 20, 1928, Amsterdam Evening Recorder, p.8. (*fultonhistory.com*)

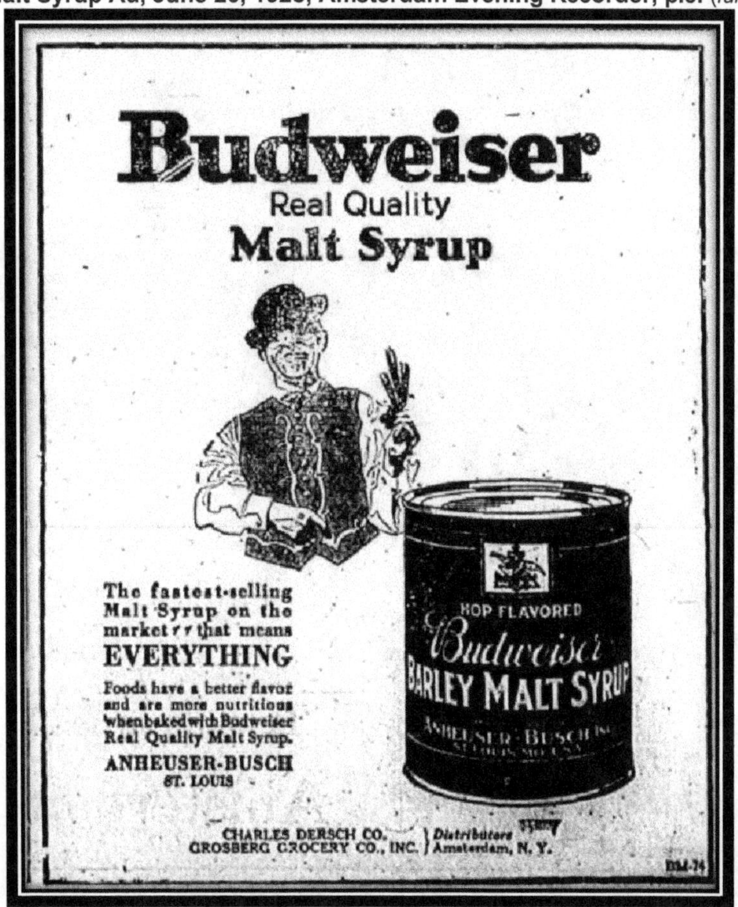

Vintage Jesso ketchup (catsup) bottle from Grosberg & Golub Company.

Assorted McCall's Meal Planner Flyers from 1940-1942 given free to shoppers in Central Market stores.

July 1941, December 1941 and January 1942, McCall's Meal Planner Flyer given free to shoppers in Central Market stores.

CENTRAL MARKET

FREE! THIS IS YOUR COPY

IT PAYS WELL TO SHOP at CENTRAL MARKET

ISSUED MONTHLY TO THE CUSTOMER FRIENDS OF CENTRAL MARKET

JULY, 1941

McCALL'S *Meal Planner*

CHOCK FULL OF ECONOMY MINDED IDEAS FOR PARTIES AND EVERYDAY MEALS

A Word to the Wise

GOOD FOOD THAT MAKES LIGHT WORK

Serve Fruits

DISH of the MONTH

WHAT I NEED

FOR PREPARED MEATS AND DELICATESSEN—TRY CENTRAL'S HIGH QUALITY AND GREATER VARIETY

Easy-Day Dessert

TIME TO REPLENISH THE JELLY SHELF

All-On-One-Plate

Easy on the Hostess

GINGER ALE

RED SALMON

CERTO

LEMON JUICE

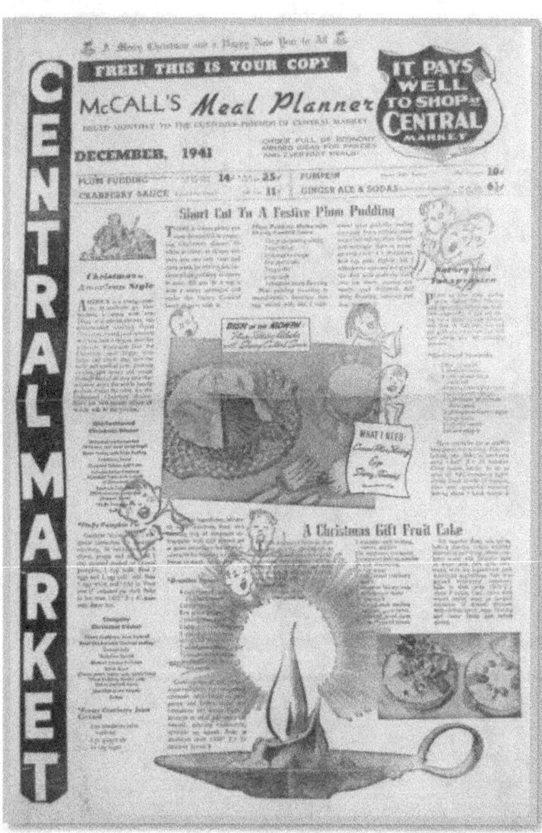

CENTRAL MARKET

FREE! THIS IS YOUR COPY

IT PAYS WELL TO SHOP at CENTRAL MARKET

McCALL'S *Meal Planner*

DECEMBER, 1941

PLUM PUDDING

CRANBERRY SAUCE

PUMPKIN

GINGER ALE & SODAS

Short Cut To A Festive Plum Pudding

DISH of the MONTH

WHAT I NEED

A Christmas Gift Fruit Cake

CENTRAL MARKET

McCALL'S

MEAL PLANNER

ISSUED MONTHLY TO THE CUSTOMER FRIENDS OF CENTRAL MARKET

CHOCK FULL OF ECONOMY MINDED IDEAS FOR PARTIES AND EVERYDAY MEALS

IT PAYS WELL TO SHOP at CENTRAL MARKET

FREE! THIS IS YOUR COPY

Savory... Substantial... and Easy on the Budget

Winter Vegetables

WHAT I NEED

MAYONNAISE

SPAGHETTI or MACARONI

COCOA

PEANUT BUTTER

Thrift Dishes That Pay High Dividends

Central Market ads, believe to have been written by Marian (Grosberg) Champagne, circa 1930s/1940s.
Courtesy Margot Champagne

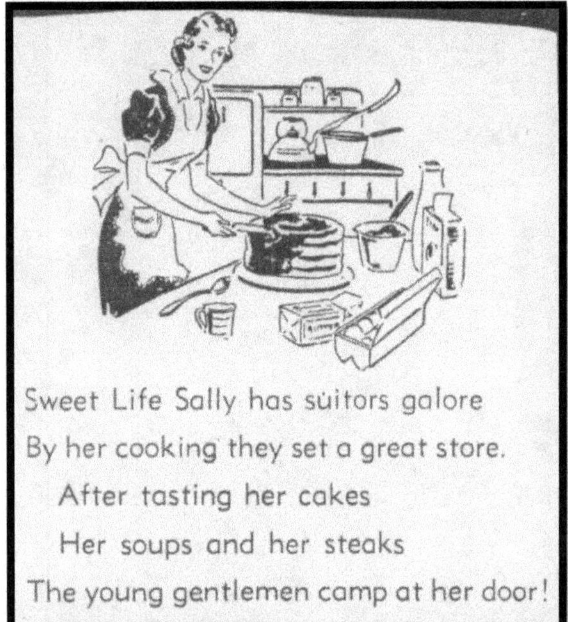

Interesting News Items

Theft

Although it often seems like life was simpler “back in the day,” crime still happened. Wholesale businesses and stores, including Grosberg’s, were occasionally targets for thieves. The following thefts to the Grosbergs’ businesses and home were reported in old newspapers:

One early incident of crime reported was for what is believed to be Joe’s father’s store in Troy. A small newspaper mention in June 1893 in the *Troy Daily Times* cites that there were warrants for the arrests of three men wanted for stealing wine from “Jacob Grosberg’s place on River Street.”

August 1921 - The Wholesale Grocery Store of Joseph E. Grosberg at 47 Van Guysling Ave was broken into. Burglars broke the lock on a driveway gate, then they forced through a belt on a rear door to gain access to the building. They entered the office, went through desks and cabinets, forcing them open by driving in the locks. They also ended up breaking open a safe by knocking off the combination knobs and then driving a machinists’ punch into the lock. They obtained $500 in cash and several hundred dollars in Liberty bonds.

December 5, 1922 - Cigarettes, tobacco and cigars stolen from warehouse of Grosberg Grocery Company 5-7 Schuyler Street. Grosberg offered a reward of $200 for information leading to the recovery of the stolen goods.

January 1923 - Grosberg Wholesale Grocery on Schuyler Street was entered by forcing open the front door. Cigars, tobacco and cigarettes were taken. Grosberg again offered a reward of $200 for information leading to the recovery of the stolen goods from both the December and January burglaries. Two people were arrested in connection with the crime, and a third person was believed to be involved.

December 1, 1924 - Grosberg Grocery store in Amsterdam was entered and robbed. Nine days later, five boys who were already on probation and were repeat offenders of various crimes were spotted by a police officer who noticed that the clothing each one was wearing was bulging. Upon investigating, the officer found the boys' clothes were stuffed with cartons of cigarettes that came from the Grosberg store. After attempting to take the boys to police headquarters, the boys all broke away from the officer but later were caught. Additional cigars and cigarettes were located in an old house belonging to the New York Central Railroad after one of the boys confessed to where they stashed the stolen goods.

February 1925 - Two men were arraigned (and pleaded not guilty) to taking cigarettes from the Grosberg Grocery Company.

June 1925 - Burglars broke into Grosberg Wholesale store house on West Main Street, Amsterdam by using a heavy hammer to break open a door. Mostly cigarettes and cigars valued at approximately $200 were taken.

Dec 1927 - The Grosberg Grocery Company warehouse was broken into and a truck belonging to the company was stolen along with a large quantity of cigars and cigarettes (40 cases valued at $1,000). The truck was recovered but the merchandise was not.

June 30, 1932 - A quantity of canned goods was stolen off a freight car on the siding to the rear of the Grosberg Grocery company in Amsterdam.

August 15, 1932 - Grosberg's warehouse at 152 West Main Street in Amsterdam was burglarized and ten cases of cigarettes, a quantity of cigars, chewing tobacco and other large quantities of tobacco were stolen.

August 1933 - Bottles of ginger ale were stolen from a warehouse of the Grosberg-Cramer Grocery Company. A 17-year-old boy and 20-year-old boy leaned through a window of the warehouse and using a long stick with a string that had a slip knot on the end were able to pull the bottles out through the window.

1935 - The Grosberg home on Union Street was robbed after burglars forced open a rear door of the house. The place was ransacked by the intruders and they made off with $75 in cash and a lady's mesh handbag.

November 1935 - The Green Island Central Market store was robbed of $2,000 when thieves blow open a safe containing money. No one heard the explosion, and it was believed that the timing of the explosion was set for when a nearby switch engine would be passing by and would camouflage the sound.[48]

These were just a sample of burglaries that appeared in newspapers, but no doubt there were many more crimes against Grosberg's businesses that didn't make the paper.

Fire

March 1916: 47 Van Guysling - fire broke out in the three-floor brick warehouse.

April 1927: 47-49 Van Guysling - same warehouse as above, now leased to Lewis Golub, but owned by Grosberg. The fire was mostly contained to the two-floor addition added on the rear of the main brick building. Water damage accounted for a great deal of the damage.

April 1948: A fire in the Grosberg-Golub Food Warehouse at 140 Erie Boulevard Fire broke out and caused serious water damage. The fire was believed to have been started by rats gnawing on matches.

Other Newsworthy Items

February 1919: A mill employee delivering a load of hay consigned to Joseph Grosberg was injured when the hay was deliberately set on fire by some boys. A passing motorist used his fire extinguisher on the flames, which gave the men time to unhitch the team of horses pulling the wagon. The mill employee climbed on top of the wagon and tried to beat some of the flames with his hands. After scourging his hands, he fell off the wagon and broke his ribs.

July 26, 1927: Two employees of the Grosberg Wholesale Grocery in Amsterdam were injured and buried up to their chests in a pile of coal while removing a partition in a coal bin in the basement of 152 West Main Street. As they were removing a partition in the coal bin, the entire partition gave way with boards falling on them and the coal spilling out up to their chests. The proprietor of the Aeillo Fruit Company at 154 West Main Street dug the men out. One man was seriously injured with a ruptured small intestine. The other man had a possible fracture to his shoulder and a severely bruised and strained leg.

Author's Note

Like many others who gave so much of themselves to help build up their community in the early 1900s, Joseph Grosberg's story was lost to time. After finding several newspaper articles mentioning Grosberg's involvement within his community, I was compelled to dig deeper. As I learned about his work and his life, I found that Joseph Grosberg played an important part in Schenectady history and championed for many Jewish causes starting in the 1920s and continuing until the end of his life. The more I discovered about him, the more I realized the importance of sharing his story so others would know the legacy he left behind. What started as a curiosity turned into an obsession. For years, I combed through thousands of newspaper articles about events or organizations that Grosberg was involved in. I obtained copies of documentation through historical groups and civic organizations that had any tidbit of information about Grosberg in their archives. I poured through old letters and journal entries of his relatives, listened to taped interviews or read written accounts that his three daughters left behind. I listened to stories and memories from his descendants and other acquaintances who knew Grosberg personally during his lifetime, and watched hours of home movies Grosberg himself had taken with his own movie camera or home movies that were taken of him. Because some of what is written here was compiled from stories passed down the Grosberg line, depending on who told the story, the details varied.

Like many research projects, the longer you work on it, the more you discover and as you discover new things, it changes the course of the story. This project could have gone on indefinitely, but after more than thirteen years researching Joseph Grosberg's life, I decided it was time to pause the research and share what I've found with those who might be interested. The history included in this book is limited to the information that was found during my research. Obviously, there is more about Grosberg's life, his work, and the businesses he founded that is not included here due to lack of available information. If you have any additional information not included, or you feel some information within this book is incorrect, please reach out to me at **csabulis@snet.net** so I can correct any errors that might have slipped through or omissions that should be added.

I am very interested in seeing any old photos with Mr. Grosberg in them, pictures of the businesses he founded, as well as old pictures of any of his family members. I would love to see photos of any pre-1940s Central Markets memorabilia you have, or anything labeled Grosberg Grocery (in Amsterdam), Grosberg-Golub, J. Grosberg & Son, or Jacob & Joseph Grosberg. If you knew Joe Grosberg personally, have any stories about him you've heard from family members, or are a distant relative of his, I'd be interested in hearing from you. You can email me at **csabulis@snet.net** or through my website **www.cindysabulis.com**.

This book is limited in distribution so if you know anyone who might be interested in purchasing a copy, I would greatly appreciate it if you would share the Amazon link to the book. I would also appreciate any mention of the book on social media sites, especially any Capital District or Schenectady groups you may belong to. Also, if you know of any descendants of the people mentioned within this book, please let them know about the book.

Acknowledgements

Many thanks to the following people for their help during this project:

- Frank Taormina and the Schenectady Historical Society.
- Marsha Jaros, Archivist at Agudat Achim Synagogue in Schenectady.
- Nanci Young, Smith College Archivist.
- Bill Buell of the *Schenectady Daily Gazette.*
- The volunteers at the Woodbridge Family History Center in Woodbridge, CT.
- Aviva Hallenstein and Andy Katz of the Schenectady Jewish Community Center.
- Carol Hamblin and other members of the Unitarian Universalist Society of Schenectady for assistance locating records regarding the history of the Delta Chi house.
- Douglas Sayles for help locating historical photos and sharing Schenectady information with me.
- Carole Bailey and John McCarthy for scouting out some ancestry.com stuff for me.
- Those who shared Grosberg information, memorabilia, and pictures, or let me pick their brains for any little tidbit of information including the Bellin family, Sylvia Mason, Margot Champagne, Susan Grosberg Bloom, Annalee Ginsberg, and Alvin Cramer Segal.
- Thomas M. Tryniski of fultonhistory.com for all the great newspapers he spends endless hours scanning and making available to the public.
- Those people who put me in touch with other people, including Marsha Axler, Caryn Wright, and Chris Cramer.
- All the Grosberg descendants and relations who shared photographs, tape recordings, written accounts, and family stories with me that helped piece together this story.

End Notes

[1] Ezekiel with an "e" is the more-common spelling, although on Joseph's 1918 WWI draft registration card it looks as if he spells his middle name Ezekial with an "a". On his draft registration in 1942 Ezekiel was spelled with an "e".

[2] Variation names and spellings include Sztabin [Pol], Shtabin [Yid, Rus], Štabinas [Lith].

[3] The surname Gans was taken from Jean M. Smith's genealogy books. Her information came from Grosberg descendants who may have made a guess at the correct spelling. One Grosberg relation listed a derivative spelling as being Gantz, and indicated that Jacob's first name was originally Morris prior to becoming Jacob Grosberg. The spelling of Jacob's parents' first and last names could also be English translated, best-guess spelling, different from the actual Hebrew, Polish, or Russian versions of their names, making it difficult to trace any early records for the Gans family back in Poland or Russia—if any survived.

[4] Champagne, Marian Grosberg, written family history, undated.

[5] Bellin, Mildred Grosberg, tape recorded interview, date unknown.

[6] Cohen, Rosalind Grosberg, Taped Interview by Ellen Robinson Epstein, Center for Oral History, Nov. 21, 1994.

[7] Bellin, Mildred Grosberg, "Rosh Hashana, 5719," *Gourmet Magazine*, Sept. 1958, pp.26-27 and pp. 56-58. Article mentions author's two grandmothers and the province they came from.

[8] "Wholesalers Blame Equalization Board for Sugar Shortage," *The Schenectady Gazette*, [Schenectady, NY], Oct. 31, 1919, p.11.

[9] "American Sugar Refining Company Sues Joseph E. Grosberg of Schenectady, N.Y. for $28,000--Defendant's Property attached.", *The American Sugar Bulletin*, May 21, 1921, Vol. 6, p.85.

[10] "Grosberg Store Not Closed by Sheriff's Order," *The Schenectady Gazette*, Schenectady, NY, May 19, 1921, p.13.

[11] Cohen, Rosalind Grosberg, Taped Interview by Ellen Robinson Epstein, Center for Oral History, Nov. 21, 1994.

[12] "Municipal Grocers' Opening Successful," *The Schenectady Gazette*, [Schenectady, NY], May 10, 1930.

[13] "Municipal Grocery Stores is Organized in Amsterdam," *Amsterdam Evening Recorder*, [Amsterdam, NY], Mar. 20, 1930, p.22.

[14] "20,000 at Food Show During Week's Exhibit," *Amsterdam Evening Recorder*, [Amsterdam, NY], Feb. 2, 1931, p.3.

[15] "Super Market on Broadway Opens Today," *The Schenectady Gazette*, Schenectady, NY, Sept. 6, 1935: p.8.

[16] Zimmerman, Max Mandell, The Super Market; A Revolution In Distribution, New York: McGraw-Hill,
1955, p.67.

[17] "Form $40,000 Firm, to Operate Huge Market," *The Schenectady Gazette*, Schenectady, NY, Jan. 17, 1935, p.4.

[18] "Broadway Home of City's Newest Food Products Outlet," *The Schenectady Gazette*, Schenectady, NY, Sept. 7, 1935, p.4.

[19] Central Market Ad, *The Schenectady Gazette*, Schenectady, NY, 1936 (month/day unknown), p4.

[20] Cohen, Rosalind Grosberg, Taped Interview by Ellen Robinson Epstein, Center for Oral History, Nov. 21, 1994.

[21] Certificate of Incorporation of The United Hebrew Community of Schenectady, Incorporated, date unknown.

[22] "Jewish Center to Construct Addition," *The Schenectady Gazette,* Schenectady, NY, May 1, 1941, p.22.
[23] "Minutes of the Schenectady Jewish Community Center Board of Directors Meeting," Sept. 3, 1957, p.2.
[24] Zimmerman, Max Mandell, The Super Market; A Revolution In Distribution, New York: McGraw-Hill, 1955, pp.71-86.
[25] Lee, Everett S., The Story of The Kiwanis Club of Schenectady, New York, Kiwanis Club of Schenectady, 1964: p.320.
[26] Ibid., pp. 308-309.
[27] "Schenectadians Need Have No Fear," *The Schenectady Gazette*, Schenectady, NY, Nov. 5, 1942, p.19.
[28] "Business Men Will Organize to Improve Traffic Conditions," The Schenectady Gazette, Schenectady, NY, April 3, 1925, p.14.
[29] "Real Estate Sales," Jacob and Anna Grosberg to Joseph Grosberg, Lot 25, Hattie Place, *The Schenectady Gazette*, [Schenectady, NY], Nov. 28, 1911, p.6.
[30] "Real Estate Sales," Joseph and Rae Grosberg, Hattie Place, *The Schenectady Gazette*, [Schenectady, NY], Aug 5, 1913, p. 5.
[31] "Real Estate Sales," Jacob Grosberg & Son, Glenville, Lot 51, Crestline Park, *The Schenectady Gazette*, [Schenectady, NY], Oct. 5, 1914, p.5.
[32] "Real Estate Sales," Jacob Grosberg and wife to Joseph Grosberg, Van Guysling Avenue Lot and S. Center Street, *The Schenectady Gazette*, [Schenectady, NY], Apr. 22, 1915.
[33] Newspaper Notice, Real Estate Transfer (47 Van Guysling Ave from Rae Grosberg to Samuel Garbowitz), *The Schenectady Gazette*, [Schenectady, NY], Dec. 19, 1935, p.6.
[34] "Cohen and Grosberg to Remodel Building," *The Schenectady Gazette*, [Schenectady, NY], May 9, 1927.
[35] "8 More Ask a Reduction in Assessment," *The Schenectady Gazette*, [Schenectady, NY], Sept. 23, 1932.
[36] Newspaper Notice, Building Permit, *The Schenectady Gazette*, [Schenectady, NY], Apr. 11, 1931, p.8.
[37] Real Estate Notice, *The Schenectady Gazette*, [Schenectady, NY], June 5, 1937, p.5.
[38] "Vintage Diner is 'Wheeled Out,'" *The Schenectady Gazette*, [Schenectady, NY], Sept. 8, 1964, p.17.
[39] State of New York Supreme Court, Appellate Division, Third Judicial Department, City of Schenectady, NY, Plaintiff-Respondent Joseph Grosberg, Samuel Scheinzeit, against Alumni Association of Union Chapter, Delta Chi Fraternity, Inc., Defendants-Appellants, p. 24.
[40] "City Gets Plans for Erie Blvd. Bus Depot," *The Schenectady Gazette,* [Schenectady, NY], May 20, 1954.
[41] "Schenectady Bus Line Franchise Sought by Canadian Firms at Sale," *Knickerbocker News*, [Albany, NY], Sept. 9, 1952, p. (unknown).
[42] "...son of Yaakov" was written in Hebrew on Joseph E. Grosberg's tombstone.
[43] "The Magistrate's Hour," *Troy Daily Times*, [Troy, NY], 1893, p (unknown).
[44] Bellin, Mildred Grosberg, "Rosh Hashana, 5719," *Gourmet Magazine*, Sep. 1958, p.26-27, 56-58.
[45] Ibid.
[46] Champagne, Marian, Quimby and Son, The Bobbs-Merrill Company, Inc., New York, 1962.
[47] Death Notice, Morris Greenblath, *The Times Record*, [Troy, NY], June 16, 1943.
[48] "Safe Blowers Get $2000 in Green Island," *The Schenectady Gazette*, [Schenectady, NY], Nov. 29, 1935, p.1/p.20.

References

Many of the newspaper articles cited here were found on the website www.fultonhistory.com. In some cases, the scanned pages on that site had dates or page numbers cut off. When that was the case, "date unknown" or "page unknown" is stated. In other cases, the page number was too dark or too grainy to see, so in those cases, best guesses were made. Those articles without any date or page number were the fault of the author for not keeping better records when first collecting material--long before the idea of composing this biography took shape.

Census Records
United State Census, Schenectady County, Schenectady, New York, Sheet No. 12-B, June 11, 1900.
United State Census, Schenectady County, Schenectady, New York, June 1, 1905.
United State Census, Schenectady County, Schenectady, New York, Sheet No.4-B, Apr. 18, 1910.
United State Census, Schenectady County, Schenectady, New York, Sheet No. 11-A, Apr. 23, 1910.
United State Census, Wayne County, Detroit, Michigan, Sheet No. 30-B, Feb. 1920.
United State Census, Schenectady County, Schenectady, New York, Sheet No. 2-B, Jan. 2-3, 1920.
United State Census, Rensselaer County, Troy, New York, Sheet No. 10-B and 11-A, Apr. 14, 1930.
United State Census, Rensselaer County, Troy, New York, Sheet No. 11-A, Apr. 14, 1930.
United State Census, Schenectady County, Schenectady, New York, Sheet No. 1-A, Apr. 2, 1930.
United State Census, Wayne County, Detroit, Michigan, Sheet No. 172-B, Apr. 24, 1930.
United State Census, Wayne County, Detroit, Michigan, Sheet No.5-A, Apr. 5, 1940.
United State Census, Wayne County, Detroit, Michigan, Sheet No.10-B, May 3, 1940.
Florida State Population Census, Precinct No. 28, Dade County, Miami, Florida, 1945.

Directories
Troy City Directories, 1897-1899.
Schenectady City Directories 1902, 1904-1905, 1907, 1909-1915, 1917-1918, 1923, 1926, 1938.

Maps
Map of Schenectady, NY, 1914.
Map of Schenectady, NY, 1917.
Map of Schenectady, NY, 1931.
Map of Schenectady, NY, 1950.

Oral Interviews
Bloom, Susan Grosberg, phone interviews with author, dates unknown.
Ginsberg, Annalee, phone interview with author, Feb. 2, 2015.
Meyer, Julie, phone interview with author, Jul. 14, 2015.
Sayles, Douglas, Schenectady History Researcher, phone interview with author, Feb. 20, 2014.
Segal, Alvin Cramer (son of George Cramer, Joseph Grosberg's business partner in his Amsterdam business), phone interview with author, Apr. 3, 2017.
Wright, Caryn, phone interview with author, Mar. 2017.

Personal Documentation
Bellin, Mildred Grosberg, tape recorded interviews, dates unknown.
Bellin, Richard A., Sr., journal entries, undated.
Champagne, Marian Grosberg, written family history, undated.
Cohen, Rosalind Grosberg, taped interview by Ellen Robinson Epstein, Center for Oral History, Nov. 21, 1994.
Grosberg, Joseph E., recorded 8mm & 16mm home movies, 1932-1956.
Smith, Jean M., "The Gans/Grosberg Family," self-printed genealogy book, undated.
Smith, Jean M., "The Greenberg Family," self-printed genealogy book, undated.
Smith, Jean M., "The Kadin/Kadisky Family," self-printed genealogy book, undated.
Smith, Jean M., "The Lasky Family," self-printed genealogy book, undated.

Businesses References

Jacob Grosberg & Son
"In City Court," (Notice of Jacob and Joseph Grosberg against Peter Ross and James Eagan, court judgment), *The Schenectady Gazette*, [Schenectady, NY], May 29, 1911, p.10.
"Personals" (Joseph Grosberg Visits Canning Factories through New Jersey and Maryland), *The Schenectady Gazette*, [Schenectady, NY], July 1914, p. 10.
"In City Court," (Legal Notice of Jacob and Joseph Grosberg against Fred Dipple), *The Schenectady Gazette*, [Schenectady, NY], Oct. 14, 1914, p.5.

"One-Way Traffic Rule Complaints Given Airing; South Center Street Merchants Tell Common Council Committee Ordinance Has Hurt Their Business—May Be Compromise to Solve Difficulty," *The Schenectady Gazette*, [Schenectady, NY], July 7, 1915.
"Fire In Schenectady," *Amsterdam Evening Recorder*, [Amsterdam, NY], Mar. 30, 1916, p.9.
"Nobody's Business, Neighborhood Gossip Among Grocers," *Trade: A Journal for Retail Merchants*, [Detroit, MI], Volume 23, Aug. 2, 1916, p. 7.
"Another Flag Raising," *The Schenectady Gazette*, [Schenectady, NY], May 16, 1917, p.2.
"Aged Woman Hit by Grocery Wagon Horse," *The Schenectady Gazette*, [Schenectady, NY], Nov. 17, 1919, p.4.
Schenectady County Unpaid Taxes List, *The Schenectady Gazette*, [Schenectady, NY], Dec. 21, 1921.
Schenectady County Unpaid Taxes List, *The Schenectady Gazette*, [Schenectady, NY], Dec. 28, 1921, p. 15.

Jacob Grosberg & Son Newspaper Advertisements

Ads for Duluth Imperial Flour, (J. Grosberg & Son Distributors), *The Schenectady Gazette*, [Schenectady, NY], June 18, 25; July 30; Aug. 6; Sept. 3, 24; Oct. 13, 22; Nov. 12, 19, 26; Dec. 3, 10, 17, & 24, 1912.
Classified Ad, Boy Over 16 Wanted, *The Schenectady Gazette*, [Schenectady, NY], Sept. 25, 1913.
Classified Ad, Driver to Deliver Groceries, *The Schenectady Gazette*, [Schenectady, NY], Aug. 1916.
Classified Ad, Man to Drive Mack Truck, *The Schenectady Gazette*, [Schenectady, NY], Oct 14, 1919, p.19.
Classified Ad, Chauffer For Truck, *The Schenectady Gazette*, [Schenectady, NY], May 4, 1920, p.17.

Grosberg Wholesale, Schenectady

"Wholesalers Blame Equalization Board for Sugar Shortage," *The Schenectady Gazette*, [Schenectady, NY], Oct. 31, 1919, p.11.
"Local Grocery Company; Grosberg Firm Incorporates in Albany for $20,000," *The Schenectady Gazette*, [Schenectady, NY], Nov. 27, 1920, p.8.
"Grosberg Store Not Closed by Sheriff's Order," *The Schenectady Gazette*, [Schenectady, NY], May 19, 1921, p.13.
"American Sugar Refining Company Sues Joseph E. Grosberg of Schenectady, N.Y. for $28,000—Defendant's Property Attached," *The American Sugar Bulletin*, May 21, 1921, Vol. 6, p.85.
"Sugar case settled," *The Schenectady Gazette*, [Schenectady, NY], May 26, 1921, p.10.
"Get $1,500 Loot, Burglars Visit Three Places at the Dorp," *Ballston Spa Daily Journal,* [Ballston, NY], Aug. 18, 1921.
"Wind Blows Sign Down," (Newspaper Notice), *The Schenectady Gazette*, [Schenectady, NY], Apr. 9, 1923.
"Exhibitors Will Draw For Places, Many Local Business Houses Will Be Represented At Schenectady Exposition," *The Schenectady Gazette*, [Schenectady, NY], Sept. 11, 1924, p.9.
"Arrest of Gregory Leads to Recovery of Many Articles," *The Schenectady Gazette*, [Schenectady, NY], Nov. 11, 1924.
"Erie Blvd. Property Is Sold in Foreclosure Suit of Lillian Cutler," *The Schenectady Gazette*, [Schenectady, NY], Feb. 20, 1930, p.2.
"Golub's Warehouse Badly Damaged by Early Morning Fire," *The Schenectady Gazette*, [Schenectady, NY], Apr. 2, 1927.
"Grocery Group Convenes," *The Leader Herald*, [Gloversville-Johnstown, NY], Nov. 11, 1930.

Grosberg Wholesale Newspaper Advertisements

Classified Ad, 2 Horses For Sale, *The Schenectady Gazette*, [Schenectady, NY], Apr. 17, 18, 19, 1923.
Classified Ads, Work Horse For Sale, *The Schenectady Gazette*, [Schenectady, NY], May 30, June 1, 2, 4, 11, 18, 21, 25, 29, July 4, 1923.
Classified Ad, Chauffer For Truck, *The Schenectady Gazette*, [Schenectady, NY], Mar. 8, 1923, p.17.
Classified Ad, Good Strong Boy Over 17 Wanted, *The Schenectady Gazette*, [Schenectady, NY], May 10, 1923, p.18.
Classified Ad, Boy Over 16 Wanted, *The Schenectady Gazette*, [Schenectady, NY], May 30-31, 1923.
Display Ad, Joseph E. Grosberg, (distributor for Budweiser Barley-Malt Syrup), *The Schenectady Gazette*, [Schenectady, NY], Apr. 3, 1930, p.13.

Grosberg Grocery, Amsterdam

Newspaper Notice, "Joseph E. Grosberg, Wholesale Grocer, is now located at 5 and 7 Schuyler Street," *Amsterdam Evening Recorder*, [Amsterdam, NY], May 1-4, 1920, p. 3/p.14.
"Joseph E. Grosberg of Schenectady is the principal stockholder of the Grosberg Grocery Company of Amsterdam," *The Schenectady Gazette*, [Schenectady, NY], Dec. 3, 1920, p.12.
"New Incorporations," *New York Times,* [New York, NY], Dec. 3, 1920, p. (unknown).
"Grocery Company Incorporated," *Amsterdam Evening Recorder*, [Amsterdam, NY], Dec. 8, 1920, p.2.
"Plunder is Soon Found by Police, Cigars and Cigarettes to Value of $800 Stolen from Grosberg Wholesale Grocery," *Amsterdam Evening Recorder*, [Amsterdam, NY], Oct. 19, 1921, p.3.
Assessor's letter in newspaper stating Grosberg Grocery is incorporated *Amsterdam Evening Recorder*, [Amsterdam, NY], Nov. 17, 1921, p.11.
"Machinists' Punch Used by Burglars," *The Schenectady Gazette*, [Schenectady, NY], Aug. 18, 1921 (morning), p. 2.

"Around The City," (Grosberg Grocery Burglarized), *Amsterdam Evening Recorder*, [Amsterdam, NY], Dec 6, 1922, p.3.
Newspaper Ad, "$200.00 Reward" (for Information leading to recovery of stolen goods), *Amsterdam Evening Recorder*, [Amsterdam, NY], Jan 31, 1923, p.8.
Newspaper Ad, "$200.00 Reward" (for Information leading to recovery of stolen goods), *Amsterdam Evening Recorder*, [Amsterdam, NY], Feb. 3, 1923, p.12.
"Charged With Robbery," (Steve Andrus for burglary of Grosberg Wholesale) *The Schenectady Gazette*, [Schenectady, NY], Feb. 3, 1923, p.2.
"Local News" (Stephen Andrus of Amsterdam arrested in robbery of Grosberg store), *The Morning Herald*, [Gloversville and Johnstown, NY], Feb (day unknown) 1923, p.10.
"Quillinan Held for Burglary," (Emery Quillinan for burglary of Grosberg Wholesale) *Amsterdam Evening Recorder*, [Amsterdam, NY], Feb. 13, 1923, p.10.
"Held on Burglary Charge," (Emery Quillinan and Stephen Andrus) *The Schenectady Gazette*, [Schenectady, NY], Feb. 14, 1923, p.10.
"Parents Surrender Son," (Steve Andrus for burglary of Grosberg Wholesale) *Fort Plain Standard*, [Fort Plain, Montgomery County, NY], Mar. 1, 1923, p.9.
Newspaper Display Ad, Notice of New Location for Grosberg Grocery Co, Inc., *Amsterdam Evening Recorder*, [Amsterdam, NY], Sept. 15, 1923.
"Paroled Boys Again In Toils" *Amsterdam Evening Recorder*, [Amsterdam, NY], Dec. 9, 1924, p.5.
"Pleads Guilty to Manslaughter," (James Draus and Alexander Koslba arraigned and pleaded not guilty/burglary suspects from Grosberg Grocery Company), *Amsterdam Evening Recorder*, [Amsterdam, NY], Feb. 14, 1925, p.3.
"St. Johnsville Man Sentenced," (Alexander Koslba pleads guilty for burglary), *Amsterdam Evening Recorder*, [Amsterdam, NY], Feb. 14, 1925, p. (unknown).
"Youth Arrested on Theft Charge, Steve Andrus Believed to be One of Three Implicated in Grosberg Burglary," *Amsterdam Evening Recorder*, [Amsterdam, NY], Feb. 14, 1925, p.3.
Newspaper Notice, Alexander Koslba Indicted For Burglary, *Amsterdam Evening Recorder*, [Amsterdam, NY], Feb. 25, 1925, p. (unknown).
"First Trial in County Court," (Alexander Koslba Sentenced For Burglary), *Amsterdam Evening Recorder*, [Amsterdam, NY], Feb. 26, 1925, p.14.
"Locust Avenue Store Robbed," *Amsterdam Evening Recorder*, [Amsterdam, NY], June 12, 1925, p.18.
"Unusual Case is Considered," *Amsterdam Evening Recorder*, [Amsterdam, NY] June 18, 1925, p.3.
"Smokers Invade Wholesale Place," *Amsterdam Evening Recorder*, [Amsterdam, NY], June 29, 1925, p.12.
"Several Sent to Institutions," (Alex Koslba committed for violating terms of probation for robbing the Grosberg store house), *Amsterdam Evening Recorder*, [Amsterdam, NY], Feb. 2, 1926, p.14.
"Workman Caught by Sliding Coal," *Amsterdam Evening Recorder*, [Amsterdam, NY], July 26, 1927.
Newspaper Notice of sale of property by Grosberg Grocery Co. Inc. on West Main Street, Amsterdam to John G. Doak and Wife, *Amsterdam Evening Recorder*, [Amsterdam, NY], Sept. 27, 1927, p.12.
"Police Hunt Clue To Grocery Theft," *Albany Evening News*, [Albany, NY], Dec. 13, 1927, s.2, p.1.
"Find Stolen Truck," *The Schenectady Gazette*, [Schenectady, NY], Dec. 13, 1927, p.2.
"Social and Personal," Joseph E. Grosberg and George Cramer attend trade conference, *Amsterdam Evening Recorder*, [Amsterdam, NY], May 24, 1928, p.3.
Newspaper Notice, Joseph E. Grosberg, Samuel Cramer, and George Cramer attend trade convention, *Amsterdam Evening Recorder*, [Amsterdam, NY], May 28, 1929, p.3.
Newspaper Notice, Grosberg Grocery membership into Amsterdam Chamber of Commerce, *Amsterdam Evening Recorder*, [Amsterdam, NY], Sept. 30, 1929.
"Around the City," (Grosberg Grocery truck in accident), *Amsterdam Evening Recorder*, [Amsterdam, NY], Feb. 28, 1930, p.3.
"Association Votes to Give Reward to Sergeant G. Flynn," *The Morning Herald*, [Gloversville and Johnstown, NY], Oct. 9, 1930, p.16.
"Groceries Taken From Freight Car," *Amsterdam Evening Recorder*, [Amsterdam, NY], June 29, 1932, p.14.
"Freight Car Robbery Probed by Officials," *The Morning Herald*, [Gloversville and Johnstown, NY], June 30, 1932, p.8.
"Freight Car Burglarized," *The Schenectady Gazette*, [Schenectady, NY], June 30, 1932, p.2.
"Grosberg Wholesale House Burglarized," *The Morning Herald*, [Gloversville and Johnstown, NY], Aug. 16, 1932, p.2.
"Firm Incorporates, *The Morning Herald*, [Gloversville and Johnstown, NY], Sept. 13, 1932.
Newspaper Notice, Grosberg Grocery, license to sell beer and wine in Albany County, *Times-Union*, [Albany, NY], July, 5, 1933, p.12.
Newspaper Notice (Burglary at Grosberg-Cramer Grocery Company,) *The Schenectady Gazette*, [Schenectady, NY], Aug. 29, 1933, p.9.
"Death Summons George Cramer," *Amsterdam Evening Recorder*, [Amsterdam, NY], Oct. 28, 1940, p. 3.
George Cramer Obituary, *The Morning Herald*, [Gloversville and Johnstown, NY], Oct. 29, 1940, p.6.
George Cramer Newspaper Funeral Notice, *Amsterdam Evening Recorder*, [Amsterdam, NY], Oct. 29, 1940, p.9.
Legal Notice: S & G Cramer Co. Name Change, *Amsterdam Evening Recorder*, [Amsterdam, NY], Dec. 17, 1940.
"Grosberg Grocery Company Changes Corporate Title," *Amsterdam Evening Recorder*, [Amsterdam, NY], Nov. 27 1943, p.3.

"Glancing Backwards Over the Recorder Files" (coal incident), *Amsterdam Evening Recorder*, [Amsterdam, NY], July 28, 1947, p.4.
"Alleged robber is arrested in Amsterdam," *The Schenectady Gazette*, [Schenectady, NY], Oct. 20, 1921, p. 10.
"Amsterdam Grocers Shut Down," *Daily Sentinel*, [Rome, NY], July 1955.
Patricia Hennessy, "Lynch's 'Depression Class' recalls Amsterdam Life in '32", *The Schenectady Gazette*, [Schenectady, NY], July 7, 1991.

Grosberg Grocery /Grosberg-Cramer Newspaper Advertisements

Joseph E. Grosberg (United States Grain Corporation Flour), *Amsterdam Evening Recorder*, [Amsterdam, NY], Feb. 9, 1920, p 2.
Floor Space to Rent, Grosberg Grocery Co., *Amsterdam Evening Recorder*, [Amsterdam, NY], Nov. 6, 13, 20, 25, 1925.
Display Ad, Grosberg Grocery (Budweiser Malt), *Amsterdam Evening Recorder*, [Amsterdam, NY], May 4, 1927, p.12.
Display Ad, Grosberg Grocery (Budweiser Malt), *Amsterdam Evening Recorder*, [Amsterdam, NY], June 1, 1927, p 9.
Display Ad, Grosberg Grocery (Budweiser Malt), *Amsterdam Evening Recorder*, [Amsterdam, NY], August 10 1927, p.5.
Classified Ad, (Help Wanted Two Advertising Campaign Men), *Amsterdam Evening Recorder*, [Amsterdam, NY], Apr. 5, 1928, p.19.
Display Ad, Grosberg Grocery (Budweiser Malt), *Amsterdam Evening Recorder*, [Amsterdam, NY], June 20, 1928, p 8.
Display Ad, Grosberg Grocery (White House Coffee), *Amsterdam Evening Recorder*, [Amsterdam, NY], Sept. 14, 1928, p.8.
Display Ad, Grosberg Grocery (Morning Sip Coffee), *Amsterdam Evening Recorder*, [Amsterdam, NY], Oct. 26, 1928.
Display Ad, Grosberg Grocery (Morning Sip Coffee), *Amsterdam Evening Recorder*, [Amsterdam, NY], Feb. 1, 1929, p. 2.
Display Ad, Grosberg Grocery (Morning Sip Coffee), *Amsterdam Evening Recorder*, [Amsterdam, NY], Feb. 15, 1929, p. 7.
Display Ad, Grosberg Grocery (Morning Sip Coffee), *Amsterdam Evening Recorder*, [Amsterdam, NY], Feb. 22, 1929, p. 10.
Display Ad, Grosberg Grocery (Budweiser Malt), *Amsterdam Evening Recorder*, [Amsterdam, NY], Sept. 5, 1929, p 9.
Display Ad, Grosberg Grocery Co., Inc., *Amsterdam Evening Recorder*, [Amsterdam, NY], Mar. 2, 1930.
Display Ad, Grosberg Grocery (Touting Exclusive Sweet Life Food Products), *Amsterdam Evening Recorder*, [Amsterdam, NY], 1931
Display Ad, Grosberg-Cramer, *The Morning Herald*, [Gloversville and Johnstown, NY], Aug. 29, 1933.
Display Ad, Grosberg-Cramer, Lang's Old German Beer, *The Morning Herald*, [Gloversville and Johnstown, NY], Aug. 31, 1933, p.11.
Display Ad, Grosberg Grocery Co., Inc., *Daily Democrat and Recorder*, [Amsterdam, NY], Sept. 18, 1931, p. 10.
Newspaper Advertisement for Sweet Life Contest, *Amsterdam Evening Recorder*, [Amsterdam, NY], Jan. 7, 1932, p.7.

Snow Baby Brand Canned Goods

"Grosberg, Joseph E., doing business as Grosberg Packing Co., Schenectady, NY." (patent for canned fruits and vegetables and spices) 169,343, June 12, Serial No. 170,683 *Index of Patents Issued from the United States Patent Office* 1923, U.S. Govt. Print. Off. [Washington, DC] published March 27, 1924, pp. 686, 882, 1441.
Logo for Snow Baby *Official Gazette of the United States Patent Office*, Volume 308, U.S. Govt. Print. Off. [Washington, DC] March 1923 pp. ix, xvii, p.683.
Newspaper Ad, Snow Baby Peas (J.S. Avery's Food Shop), *Ballston Spa Daily Journal*, [Ballston, NY], Apr. 27, 1923, p. (unknown).
Newspaper Ad, Snow Baby Brand Peas and Tomatoes (The Carl Co.), *The Schenectady Gazette*, [Schenectady, NY], May 25, 1923, p. (unknown).
Newspaper Ad, Snow Baby Brand Peas and Tomatoes (The Carl Co.), *The Schenectady Gazette*, [Schenectady, NY], Oct. 15, 1923, p.5.
Newspaper Ad, Snow Baby Tomatoes, *The Schenectady Gazette*, [Schenectady, NY], July 17, 1925, p.17.
Newspaper Ad, Snow Baby Corn (Jos. E. Grosberg), *The Schenectady Gazette*, [Schenectady, NY], Aug. 26, 1925, p.11.
Newspaper Ad, Snow Baby Corn, (B. Yanover), *The Schenectady Gazette*, [Schenectady, NY], Apr. 16, 1926, p.8.
Newspaper Ad, Snow Baby Tomatoes and Corn (Yanover's), *The Schenectady Gazette*, [Schenectady, NY], Apr. 23, 1926, p. (unknown).
Newspaper Ad, Snow Baby Catsup and Sauerkraut (Municipal Grocery Stores), *Amsterdam Evening Recorder*, [Amsterdam, NY], March 28, 1930, p.6.

Newspaper Ad, Snow Baby Sauerkraut, (Robert F. Leslie) *Morning Herald* [Gloversville and Johnstown, NY], March 28, 1930, p.8.
Newspaper Ad, Snow Baby Tomatoes, (Municipal Grocery Stores), *The Saratogian,* [Saratoga, NY], Apr. 24, 1930, p. 8.
Newspaper Ad, Snow Baby Sauerkraut and Dried Beef, (Municipal Grocery Stores), *The Saratogian,* [Saratoga, NY], May 1, 1930, p.7.
Newspaper Ad, Snow Baby brand (Municipal Grocery Stores), *The Schenectady Gazette*, [Schenectady, NY], Aug. 15, 1930, p.4.
Newspaper Ad, Snow Baby Ammonia, (Municipal Grocery Stores), *Fort Plain Standard*, [Fort Plain, NY], Sept. 4, 1930, p.5.
Newspaper Ad, Snow Baby Sliced Beef, (Municipal Grocery Stores), *Amsterdam Evening Recorder*, [Amsterdam, NY], Sept. 11, 1930, p.9.
Newspaper Ad, Snow Baby Sauerkraut, (Municipal Grocery Stores), *Fort Plain Standard*, [Fort Plain, NY], Sept. 25, 1930, p.5.
Newspaper Ad, Snow Baby Sliced Beef, (Municipal Grocery Stores), *Amsterdam Evening Recorder*, [Amsterdam, NY], Oct. 9, 1930. p.8.
Newspaper Ad, Snow Baby Sauerkraut, (Municipal Grocery Stores), *The Saratogian,* [Saratoga, NY], Oct. 13, 1930, p.12.

Grosberg-Golub

"Wholesale Grocery Houses of Grosberg and Golub Combine," *The Schenectady Gazette*, [Schenectady, NY], Feb. 12, 1930, p.7.
"Golub Grosberg Firm to be known as G.G. Grocery Co." *The Schenectady Gazette*, [Schenectady, NY], Feb. 14, 1930.
"Funeral Services Are Held for Lewis Golub, Well Known Resident, *The Schenectady Gazette*, [Schenectady, NY], Feb. 17, 1930, p. 14.
"Schenectady Grocery Concerns in Merger," *Albany Times-Union*, [Albany, NY], Feb. 13, 1930, s.2, p.1.
"2 Schenectady Firms Chartered by State," *The Schenectady Gazette*, [Schenectady, NY], July 3, 1930, p.12.
"Local Grocery Raises Capital," *The Schenectady Gazette*, [Schenectady, NY], July 15, 1930, p.4.
"Local Grocery Firm Has Changed Name," *The Schenectady Gazette*, [Schenectady, NY], Jan. 12, 1931.
"City Court Judgments," *The Schenectady Gazette*, [Schenectady, NY], Mar. 16, 1931, p.5.
"Wholesalers Are Back From Meet," *The Schenectady Gazette*, [Schenectady, NY], Feb. 1, 1932, p. 11.
Newspaper Mention, John George takes position of traveling salesman, *The Saratogian* [Saratoga, NY], Jan. 25, 1932, p.8.
"77 Industries Represented by City's Recovery Board," *The Schenectady Gazette*, [Schenectady, NY], July 27, 1933, p. 4.
"Local Food Firm Obtains Branch at Glens Falls," *The Schenectady Gazette*, [Schenectady, NY], 1934 date (unknown), p. (unknown).
"Grosberg, Golub Co. Officials Are Guests Of Honor," *The Schenectady Gazette*, [Schenectady, NY], 1935.
"250 Employees Guests at Party for Grosberg" *The Schenectady Gazette*, [Schenectady, NY], Dec. 27, 1935, p.5.
"Employees Pay Golub Tribute," *The Schenectady Gazette*, [Schenectady, NY], Mar. 3, 1936, p.9.
Newspaper Notice, Grosberg & Golub, Co., license to sell beer at 14th St. and Broadway, Watervliet, *Cohoe's American* [Cohoes, NY], July 31, 1936, p.12.
Newspaper Notice, Grosberg & Golub, Inc. license to sell beer at Paine and Swan Streets, Green Island, *Ibid.*
Newspaper Notice, Grosberg & Golub, Inc. license to sell beer in Saratoga Springs, *The Saratogian*, [Saratoga Springs, NY], Aug. 12, 1936, p.13.
Newspaper Legal Notice, 100 Cans of Tomato Paste Seized from Grosberg-Golub, *Times-Union*, [Albany, NY], Dec. 28, 1939, p.18.
"Sandwich Spread Action Settled," *Knickerbocker News* [Albany, NY], July 27, 1942, p.3.
Property Transfer Notice, Central Market, Inc. to Grosberg-Golub, *Times-Union*, [Albany, NY], May 7, 1941, p.13.
"District Grocers Elect Bernard Golub," *The Schenectady Gazette*, [Schenectady, NY], June 12, 1943, p (unknown).
"Local Firms In District Grocers' Assn.," *The Schenectady Gazette*, [Schenectady, NY], June 26, 1943, p.22.
"Local Food Distributors Form Council," *The Schenectady Gazette*, [Schenectady, NY], June 10, 1943, p.13.
"Hundreds Fete Grosberg at Dinner, Dance," *The Schenectady Gazette*, [Schenectady, NY], Nov. 23, 1943, p.9.
"Market Head Retires," *Troy Record*, [Troy, NY], Oct 25 1943, p.2.
"What's Doing in Nearby Towns," (Joseph E. Grosberg, president of Central Markets, Inc., and Grosberg-Golub. wholesale grocers retires), The Leader-Republican, [Gloversville and Johnstown], NY, Oct. 23, 1943, p. 3.
"Market Head Retires," *The Troy Record*, [Troy, NY], Oct. 25. 1943, p.(unknown).
"Grosberg, Executive of Grocery Firm Retires", *The Schenectady Gazette*, [Schenectady, NY], Oct. 23, 1943.
"Golub Elected Director Of Market Institute," *The Schenectady Gazette*, [Schenectady, NY], June 26, 1944, p.13.
"Name of City Concern Changed by Owners," *The Schenectady Gazette*, [Schenectady, NY], Aug. 26, 1944, p. (unknown).
"Rats Gnawing On Matches Cause Fire; Serious Water Damage Results at Food Warehouse of Grosberg-Golub, Inc." Apr. 5, 1948.
"Golubs, Central Markets Founders, Feted at Testimonial Dinner," *The Schenectady Gazette*, [Schenectady, NY], Nov. 1, 1957, p. 25.

Judgements Satisfied, Grosberg-Golub Co. vs. Abraham B. Goldsmith, *The Schenectady Gazette*, [Schenectady, NY], date (unknown), 1934, p. (unknown).

Double GG Newspaper Advertisements

Double GG, (distributors for Budweiser Barley-Malt Syrup), *The Schenectady Gazette*, [Schenectady, NY], Apr. 17, 1930, p.13.
Double GG, (distributors for Budweiser Barley-Malt Syrup), *The Schenectady Gazette*, [Schenectady, NY], May 28, 1930, p.25.
Double GG, (distributors for Budweiser Barley-Malt Syrup), *The Schenectady Gazette*, [Schenectady, NY], June, 1930, p.27.
Double GG, (distributors for Budweiser Barley-Malt Syrup), *The Schenectady Gazette*, [Schenectady, NY], June 25, 1930, p.27.
Double GG, (distributors for Budweiser Barley-Malt Syrup), *The Schenectady Gazette*, [Schenectady, NY], July 10, 1930, p.12.
Double GG, (distributors for Budweiser Barley-Malt Syrup), *The Schenectady Gazette*, [Schenectady, NY], July 31, 1930, p.18.
Double GG, (distributors for Budweiser Barley-Malt Syrup), *The Schenectady Gazette*, [Schenectady, NY], Aug. 6, 1930, p.17.
Double GG, (distributors for Budweiser Barley-Malt Syrup), *The Schenectady Gazette*, [Schenectady, NY], Aug. 14, 1930, p.18.
Double GG, (distributors for Budweiser Barley-Malt Syrup), *The Schenectady Gazette*, [Schenectady, NY], Oct. 24, 1930, p.35.

Grosberg-Golub Newspaper Advertisements

Municipal Stores and Sweet Life Canned Fruit, *The Schenectady Gazette*, [Schenectady, NY], Apr. 10, 1931, p. (unknown).
Sweet Life Ad with Free Theater Ticket Offer, *The Schenectady Gazette*, [Schenectady, NY], May 24, 1933, p.11.
Classified Ad, Lost & Found: Lost Roll of City Charity Slips, *The Schenectady Gazette*, [Schenectady, NY], Aug. 1, 1936, p.18.
Classified Ad, Men for Warehouse Work, *The Schenectady Gazette*, [Schenectady, NY], Nov. 18, 1942, p.20.
Classified Ad, Girls Wanted for Self-Serve Market, *The Schenectady Gazette*, [Schenectady, NY], Nov. 18, 1942, p.26.
Classified Ad, Clerical Office Worker, *The Schenectady Gazette*, [Schenectady, NY], Dec. 31, 1942, p.21.
Classified Ad, Men for Warehouse Work, *The Schenectady Gazette*, [Schenectady, NY], Apr. 3, 1943, p.29.
Classified Ad, Young Men for Warehouse Work and Bookkeeper, *The Schenectady Gazette*, [Schenectady, NY], March 8, 1944, p.18.
Classified Ad, Young Men for Warehouse Work, *The Schenectady Gazette*, [Schenectady, NY], Mar. 14, 1944, p.14.
Classified Ad, Chauffer, *The Schenectady Gazette*, [Schenectady, NY], Aug. 31, 1944, p.19.

Central Markets

"Grocery Chain Head Is Full Of Optimism," *The Schenectady Gazette*, [Schenectady, NY], Jan. 7, 1931.
Newspaper notice regarding dumping of refuse behind Public Service Market, *The Troy Times*, [Troy, NY], Apr. 25, 1933.
"Mayor Urges Three Market Groups Join Drive for U.S. Funds," *Albany Times-Union* [Albany, NY], Feb. 18, 1934, B-1.
"Birthday Sale at Big Market," *The Schenectady Gazette*, [Schenectady, NY], Sept. 28, 1934.
"Police Investigating Robbery at Central Market" *The Troy Times*, [Troy, NY], Nov 1, 1934, p.2.
"Market Firm Workers Have Dinner Dance," *The Schenectady Gazette*, [Schenectady, NY], Oct. (day unknown) 1934, p.(unknown).
"Broadway Once Known as a Residential Area," *The Schenectady Gazette*, [Schenectady, NY], Sept. 28, 1934.
"Super Market on Broadway Opens Today," *The Schenectady Gazette*, [Schenectady, NY], Sept. 6, 1935, p.8.
"Store Workers to Meet," *The Schenectady Gazette*, [Schenectady, NY], Sept. 16, 1935, p. 3.
"Central Market Employees Hold Holiday Dance," *The Schenectady Gazette*, [Schenectady, NY], Oct. 31, 1935.
"Safe Blowers Get $2000 in Green Island," *The Schenectady Gazette*, [Schenectady, NY], Nov. 29, 1935, p.1/p.20.
"Central Market Robbed of $2000 as Safe Cracked," *The Times Record*, [Troy, NY], Dec 30, 1935, p. 22.
"New Owners For Central Market," *The Morning Herald*, [Gloversville and Johnstown, NY], July 3, 1936, p.14.
"Awards Market Contest Prize," *The Schenectady Gazette*, [Schenectady, NY], Sept. 14, 1936, p. 5.
"Central market heads and Wives at Dinner Meet," *The Schenectady Gazette*, [Schenectady, NY], Oct. 1936.
"City Merchants on Buying Trip," *The Schenectady Gazette*, [Schenectady, NY], Jan. 26, 1937, p.22.
"Central Fruit Market Men Meet at Annual Dinner," *The Schenectady Gazette*, [Schenectady, NY], Apr. 8, 1937, p.12.
"Voice of Central Markets Program Attracts Food-Buying Audience," *WGY (NBC) News,* Schenectady, NY, May, 1937, Volume 2, Number 4.
"Snyder Enters Agreement with N.Y.P.L. Ass'n," *The Schenectady Gazette*, [Schenectady, NY], July 20, 1937, p. 2.

"Traction Union Maps New Pact," (Warehouse Employees of Central Markets), *The Schenectady Gazette*, [Schenectady, NY], July 27, 1937.

"Drinking 50 Carloads of Milk Not Impossible Task, Says Grosberg," *The Schenectady Gazette*, [Schenectady, NY], Sept. 17, 1937, p.8.

"Schenectady Homes of Central Market," (photos) *The Schenectady Gazette*, [Schenectady, NY], Sept. 17, 1937, p.23.

"Special Values In Fresh Fruit and Vegetables," *Ibid.*

"Reasons Why Markets Are Popular Given," *Ibid.*

"Month's Sale Starts Today at Central 'Marts'," *Ibid.*

"Joseph E. Grosberg Returns From Coast," *Ibid.*

"Buying Policy Factor in Rapid Gain of Stores," *Ibid.*

"Food Markets Employees Vote 6pm closing" *The Schenectady Gazette*, [Schenectady, NY], Sept. 17, 1937.

"Two Bandits Used Ladder to Enter Central Market," *The Times Record*, [Troy, NY], Oct. 3, 1937, p. (unknown).

"Central markets Now Largest Retail Outlet for Produce in Eastern N.Y., Says Department Head," Sept. 17, 1937.

"Food Market Employees Win 48 Hour Week," *The Schenectady Gazette*, [Schenectady, NY], Sept. 22, 1937, p. 11.

"Saturday Night Closing Agreed by Food Group," *The Schenectady Gazette,* [Schenectady, NY], Sept. 24, 1937.

"Troy Area Police Coming Section for Armed Pair," *The Times Record*, [Troy, NY], Oct. 4, 1937, p.9.

"Store Workers Open Parley to Increase Wage," *The Schenectady Gazette*, [Schenectady, NY], Oct. 26, 1937.

"Store Workers Given Contract," *Times Union*, [Albany, NY], Oct. 30, 1937.

"Anniversary of Central Market Being Celebrated," *The Times Record*, [Troy, NY], (date unknown) 1937, p.3.

Legal Notice: Grosberg-Golub Corp misbranded canned peas, *The Schenectady Gazette*, [Schenectady, NY], Apr. 6, 1938, p.22.

"Marshmallows Bought in Tons," *The Schenectady Gazette*, [Schenectady, NY], Apr. 8, 1938, p.12.

"Area Employees of Central Markets Meet At Dinner," *The Schenectady Gazette*, [Schenectady, NY], Apr. 14, 1938.

"Central Market To Open Third Big Unit Today," *The Schenectady Gazette*, [Schenectady, NY], May 18, 1938.

"To Inaugurate New Type of Food Market," *The Schenectady Gazette*, [Schenectady, NY], May 30, 1933, p.2.

"Central Markets Host to Employees at Annual Outing," *The Schenectady Gazette*, [Schenectady, NY], July 19, 1938.

"New Marketing Center To Open," *The Schenectady Gazette*, [Schenectady, NY], Aug. 8, 1938, p.4.

"2 Schenectady Homes of Central Market," *The Schenectady Gazette*, [Schenectady, NY], Sept. 16, 1938, p.16.

"Central Markets Celebrate Sixth Anniversary Date," *Ibid.*

"Newest Central Market on Broadway," (photo), *Ibid.*

"Central Market Starts a "Month of Value Sale"," *Ibid.*

"Buying Policy Factor in Rapid Gain of Stores, *Ibid.* (same article published in Sept. 17, 1937 issue).

"Reasons Why Markets Are Popular Given," *Ibid.* (same article published in Sept. 17, 1937 issue).

"Special Values In Fresh Fruit and Vegetables," *Ibid.* (same article published in Sept. 17, 1937 issue).

"New Central Market Opens Today at 331 Columbia," *Utica Daily Press*, [Utica, NY], Nov. 11, 1938, p. 4.

Newsletter mention, Grosberg-Golub sign renewal order for 52 weeks, *WGY (NBC) News,* Schenectady, NY, Jan. 1939, Volume 4, Number 1.

"Central Market Opens Its 12th Area store," *Times-Union*, [Albany, NY], Feb. 7, 1941.

"Mayor Opens New Albany Market," *Knickerbocker News*, [Albany, NY], Feb. 6, 1941, p10B.

"Market Chain Opens New Unit," *The Schenectady Gazette*, [Schenectady, NY], Feb. 14, 1941, p.6.

"New Central Market Opens In Broadway," *The Saratogian*, [Saratoga Springs, NY], June 10, 1942.

"Fire Wrecks Food Mart on Eastern Parkway," *The Schenectady Gazette*, [Schenectady, NY], Oct. 10, 1942, p.1.

"Schenectady Fire Damages Market," *The Knickerbocker News*, [Albany, NY], Oct. 10, 1942, s.2, p.1.

"Remodeled Central Market Reopens For Business," *The Schenectady Gazette*, [Schenectady, NY], Nov 25, 1942.

"Announces Reopening," *The Schenectady Gazette*, [Schenectady, NY], 1942 date (unknown).

"Battalion Chief Injures Foot At Fire In South End," (Fire At Central Market Jackson St), *The Times Record*, [Troy, NY], Jan. 11, 1943, p.3.

Obituary Notice, Henry Diamond, (Central Market fruits and vegetable manager), *The Times Record*, [Troy, NY], July 24, 1944, p.2

"No-Cause Verdict at Ballston Court in Hotaling Action," (Central Markets sued for injuries), *The Times Record*, [Troy, NY], Feb. 5, 1945, p.5.

"Get New Positions," (photo--manager of DeFreest Dept. Store), *The Schenectady Gazette*, [Schenectady, NY], Jan. 6, 1948, p.20.

"4 Promoted In Golub Store Chain," *Knickerbocker News*, [Albany, NY], Jan. 6, 1948, p.12B.

"Gunmen Escape with $6,000 from Central Market," *The Times Record*, [Troy, NY], Apr. 21, 1951, p.1.

"Hugh McCartney Former Grocery Operator Dies," The Evening Leader, [Corning, NY], July 2, 1952, p.1.

"New Central Market Opens Tomorrow," *The Times Record*, [Troy, NY], Dec. 14, 1953, p.40.

"Note Central Markets 25 Years," *The Times Record*, [Troy, NY], Nov. 2, 1957, p. 5.

"Central Markets 25 Years Old," *Knickerbocker News*, [Albany, NY], 1957, p.B12.

"Central Markets Founded In Green Island," *The Troy Record*, [Troy, NY], Oct. 28, 1958, p. 26.

"Warehouse Facilities of Central Market Corp. Enlarged," Glens Falls Times, [Glens Falls, NY], May 29, 1969, p.23.

"Central Market Plans 20 New Supermarkets in Five Years" *Albany Times-Union,* [Albany, NY], June 22, 1969, p.F-2.

"Central Market Corp. Enlarges Facilities," *The Post-Star*, [Glens Falls, NY], May 31, 1969, p. 14.

"Saga of Central Markets Is Told to Press," *The Leader-Herald*, [Gloversville and Johnstown, N Y], June 5, 1969, p. 7.
"Central Markets Saga Started in Single Store," *The Record Newspapers*, [Troy NY], Jan. 30, 1970, B-4.
"Saga of Central Markets Started in Single Store," *The Record Newspapers*, [Troy NY], Jan. 28, 1972, B-28.
"Then & Now: Albany, the South Mall and a Neighborhood Lost," https://www.albanycountyny.gov/home/showpublisheddocument/328/636982284110070000

Public Service Market Newspaper Advertisements

Green Island Public Service Economy Center, *Cohoes American,* [Cohoes, NY], Mar. 23, 1933, p.6.
Green Island Public Service Economy Center, *Cohoes American,* [Cohoes, NY], Apr. 13, 1933, p.7.
Green Island Public Service Economy Center, *The Troy Times,* [Troy, NY], Apr. 25, 1933, p.14.
Public Service Economy/Watervliet Central Cash Market, *The Troy Times,* [Troy, NY], Wednesday Evening, Nov. 22 and Friday Evening, Nov. 24, 1933, p.6.
Public Service Market/Central Market, *The Troy Times*, [Troy, NY], Jan. 26, 1934, p. 6.
Public Service Market/Central Market, *The Times Record*, [Troy NY], May 28, 1934.
Public Service Economy Market/Central Market, *The Times Record*, [Troy NY], June 15, 1934, p.6.
Public Service Economy Market /Watervliet Central Market, *The Troy Times*, [Troy, NY], July 20, 1934, p.2.

Central Market Newspaper Advertisements

Central Market, "Thrifty Housewives of Schenectady," *The Schenectady Gazette*, [Schenectady, NY], July 28, 1933.
Central Market, *The Schenectady Gazette*, [Schenectady, NY], Aug. 5, 1933.
Central Market, *The Schenectady Gazette*, [Schenectady, NY], Aug. 4, 1933, p. 21.
Central Market, *The Schenectady Gazette*, [Schenectady, NY], Apr. 19, 1934, p.2.
Central Market (regarding food shortages), *The Schenectady Gazette*, [Schenectady, NY], Sep. 15, 1934, p.4.
Central Market, *Post-Star*, [Glens Falls, NY], Nov 12, 1935, p.3.
The Super Market, Broadway & Hamilton St., *The Schenectady Gazette*, [Schenectady, NY], Nov. 27, 1936, p. 12.
Central Market, *The Schenectady Gazette*, [Schenectady, NY], 1936 (month/date unknown), p.4.
Central Market Cooking School, *The Schenectady Gazette*, [Schenectady, NY], June 13, 1938, p.2.
Central Market Cooking School *The Schenectady Gazette*, [Schenectady, NY], June 27, 1938, p. 2.
Central Market, *The Schenectady Gazette*, [Schenectady, NY], July 15, 1938.
Central Market, *The Schenectady Gazette*, [Schenectady, NY], Apr. 13, 1939, p. 4.
Central Market, *The Schenectady Gazette*, [Schenectady, NY], Aug. 30, 1940.
Central Market, *The Schenectady Gazette*, [Schenectady, NY], Jan. 5, 1940, p. 4.
Central Market, *The Schenectady Gazette*, [Schenectady, NY], June 6, 1941, p. 4.
Central Market, *Knickerbocker News*, [Albany, NY], Feb. 6, 1941, B-10.
Central Market, *The Times Record*, [Troy, NY], Feb. 7, 1941, p. 21.
Central Market, *The Times Record*, [Troy, NY], Apr. 15, 1942.
Central Market, *The Schenectady Gazette*, [Schenectady, NY], Nov. 24, 1942, p. 4.
Central Market reopening, *The Schenectady Gazette*, [Schenectady, NY], Nov. 24, 1942, p4.
Central Department Store/Central Market, *The Times Record*, [Troy, NY], June 22, 1944.
Central Market, *The Times Record*, [Troy, NY], Nov. 2, 1944, p. 19.
Central Department Store, *Knickerbocker News*, [Albany, NY], Nov. 8, 1944, 8-A.
Central Department Store, *Knickerbocker News*, [Albany, NY], Nov. 30, 1944, p6-B.
Central Department Store/Central Market, *Knickerbocker News*, [Albany, NY], Nov. 30, 1944, B-6.
Central Department Store, *Knickerbocker News*, [Albany, NY], Apr. 3, 1946, B-3.
Central Market, *Knickerbocker News*, [Albany, NY], Dec 11, 1947, B-8.
Central Market "Grand Reopening Sale!" *The Schenectady Gazette*, [Schenectady, NY], Aug. 10, 1949.

Price Chopper

"William Golub to Receive B'nai B'rith Award," *The Schenectady Gazette*, [Schenectady, NY], Apr. 28, 1963, p. 11.
"Benard Golub Dies; Trade, Civic Leader," *The Schenectady Gazette*, [Schenectady, NY], May 19, 1972, p. 25.
"Price Chopper Continues to Market Itself," *Albany Times-Union*, [Albany, NY], Mar. 5, 2000.
Wechsler, Alan, "A Family Affair; As Price Chopper turns 75, the Golub clan celebrates four generations of success," *Albany Times-Union*, [Albany, NY], Nov. 11, 2007.
Boss, Donna, "A Family in Business," *Supermarket News*, Nov. 26, 2007, https://www.supermarketnews.com/retail-amp-financial/family-business.
Buell, Bill, Historic Schenectady County: A Bicentennial History, Historical Publishing Network, San Antonio, TX, 2009, pp. 84-86.
Shiro, Peg, "Price Chopper's Story Is A Family One," Nov. 15, 1990, p. T14. http://alb.merlinone.net/mweb/wmsql.wm.request?oneimage&imageid=5571740

Municipal Grocery Stores, Inc. 1930-1932

"Independent Grocery Stores to Form Chain Distributing System," *The Schenectady Gazette*, [Schenectady, NY], Feb. 21, 1930, p.14.
"Municipal Grocery Stores is Organized in Amsterdam," *Amsterdam Evening Recorder*, [Amsterdam, NY], Mar. 20, 1930, p.22.

"New Chain of 30 Grocery Stores Will Open in City This Morning," *The Schenectady Gazette*, [Schenectady, NY], May 9, 1930, p.15.
"Municipal Grocers' Opening Successful," *The Schenectady Gazette*, [Schenectady, NY], May 10, 1930, p.7.
"Amsterdam Plans Food Show at State Armory in January," *Amsterdam Evening Recorder*, [Amsterdam, NY], Nov. 8. 1930, p.5.
"Cramer Explains Municipal Plan," *Amsterdam Evening Recorder*, [Amsterdam, NY], Jan. 29, 1931, p.13.
"Amsterdam's First Food Show Opens Monday Evening," *Amsterdam Evening Recorder*, [Amsterdam, NY], Jan. 24, 1931, p.2.
"Receipts of Today's Food Show to Swell Relief Fund; Grocers and Exhibitors Join in Relief Movement," *Amsterdam Evening Recorder*, [Amsterdam, NY], Jan. 31, 1931, p.12.
"20,000 at Food Show During Week's Exhibit," *Amsterdam Evening Recorder*, [Amsterdam, NY], Feb. 2, 1931, p.3.
"Have Active Part in Directing Annual Outing of Municipal Grocery Stores," *Amsterdam Evening Recorder*, [Amsterdam, NY], July 22, 1931, p.14.
"Local Grocers Enjoy Banquet," *Amsterdam Evening Recorder*, [Amsterdam, NY], Apr. 16, 1931.
"Prominent Speaker for Grocers' Dinner," *Amsterdam Evening Recorder*, [Amsterdam, NY], Mar. 30, 1932, p.7.
"Grocers Enjoy Annual Dinner," *Amsterdam Evening Recorder*, [Amsterdam, NY], Apr. 1, 1932, p.4.
Newspaper Ad, Congratulations on Completion of a New, Modern Municipal Food Market, *The Schenectady Gazette*, [Schenectady, NY], May 7, 1932, p. 6.

Municipal Grocery Stores Newspaper Advertisements

Business Opportunities, *Brooklyn Daily Eagle*, [New York, NY], 1929.
Municipal Grocery Stores, *Amsterdam Evening Recorder*, [Amsterdam, NY], Mar. 22, 1930, p15.
Municipal Grocery Stores, *The Schenectady Gazette*, [Schenectady, NY], May 2, 1930, p.12.
Municipal Grocery Stores, *The Schenectady Gazette*, [Schenectady, NY], May 9, 1930, p.12.
Municipal Grocery Stores, *Knickerbocker News*, [Albany, NY], May 9, 1930, p.21.
Municipal Grocery Stores, *The Schenectady Gazette*, [Schenectady, NY], May 23, 1930, p. 19.
Municipal Grocery Stores, *The Schenectady Gazette*, [Schenectady, NY], July 25, 1930, p. 13.
Municipal Grocery Stores, *Amsterdam Evening Recorder*, [Amsterdam, NY], Jan. 26, 1931, p.9.
Municipal Grocery Stores, *Amsterdam Evening Recorder*, [Amsterdam, NY], Jan. 1931, p.12.
Municipal Grocery Stores, *Amsterdam Evening Recorder*, [Amsterdam, NY], Jan. 29, 1931, p.12.
Municipal Grocery Stores, *Amsterdam Evening Recorder*, [Amsterdam, NY], June 25, 1931, p.8.
Municipal Grocery Stores, *The Schenectady Gazette*, [Schenectady, NY], Dec. 23, 1930, p. (unknown).
Municipal Grocery Stores, *Amsterdam Evening Recorder*, [Amsterdam, NY], Apr. 23, 1931, p11.
Municipal Grocery Stores, *The Schenectady Gazette*, [Schenectady, NY], Aug. 21, 1931, p.13.
Municipal Grocery Stores, *The Schenectady Gazette*, [Schenectady, NY], Dec. 4, 1931, p.28.
Municipal Grocery Stores, *Amsterdam Evening Recorder*, [Amsterdam, NY], Jan. 21, 1932, p8.

Supermarkets, Inc.

"Form $40,000 Firm, to Operate Huge Market," *The Schenectady Gazette*, [Schenectady, NY], Jan. 17, 1935, p.4.
"Broadway Home of City's Newest Food Products Outlet," *The Schenectady Gazette*, [Schenectady, NY], Sept. 7, 1935, p.4.
"Super Market Begins Second Year Business," *The Schenectady Gazette*, [Schenectady, NY], May 22, 1936, p. 21.
"Finest Merchandising Mart in District Is Super's Ideal," *The Schenectady Gazette*, [Schenectady, NY], June 11, 1937, p.14.
"Super Markets Open Broadway Service Center," *The Schenectady Gazette*, [Schenectady, NY], May 14, 1938, p.7.
"Market's Expansion Is Example of Progressive Efforts," *The Schenectady Gazette*, [Schenectady, NY], Sept. 30, 1938, p.15.
"Fire Destroys Glens Falls Market," *The Saratogian*, [Saratoga Springs, NY], Nov. 30, 1944, p.11.
"Original Super Market Opens New Addition," *The Schenectady Gazette*, [Schenectady, NY], Nov. 12, 1948, p.26.
"New Supermarket Begun on State Street," *The Schenectady Gazette*, [Schenectady, NY], Aug. 8, 1951, p.33.
"Market Brings Suit," *The Schenectady Gazette*, [Schenectady, NY], Dec. 29, 1953, S2, p.1.
"Max Cohn, Market Firm Head, Dies," *The Times Record*, [Troy, N Y], Feb. 7, 1959, p.9.
"Max Cohen Dies at 74; Supermarket Originator," *Knickerbocker News*, [Albany, NY], Feb. 9, 1959, p.10B.
"Max Cohen Dies: Headed Food Market," *Albany Times Union*, [Albany, NY], Feb. 8, 1959, p. B-1.
"Max Cohn Funeral to Be Held Today," *The Schenectady Gazette*, [Schenectady, NY], Feb. 10, 1959, p.13.
"Cohn, Super Market Pioneer, Dies at 64(*sic*)," *The Schenectady Gazette*, [Schenectady, NY], Feb. 9, 1959, p. 13.

Supermarkets, Inc. Newspaper Advertisements

Supermarkets, Inc., *The Schenectady Gazette*, [Schenectady, NY], Sept. 6 1935, p.12.
Supermarkets, Inc., *The Schenectady Gazette* (morning), [Schenectady, NY], Oct. 9 1936, p.10.
Supermarkets, Inc., *The Schenectady Gazette*, [Schenectady, NY], June 11, 1937, p.11.
Supermarkets, Inc., *The Schenectady Gazette*, [Schenectady, NY], Sept. 10, 1937, p.18.

Supermarket Institute and Industry

"Super Market Institute Meets," *The Schenectady Gazette*, [Schenectady, NY], Oct. 6, 1937, p.21.
"Super Market Institute Elects Director," *The Saratogian,* [Saratoga Springs, NY], Oct. 15, 1942, p. (unknown).

Zimmerman, M. M., The Super Market; A Revolution In Distribution, New York: McGraw-Hill, 1955.

Frank's Economy Store
"Cooper Realty buys Frank's Store Bldgs," *Burlington Free Press* [Burlington, VT], Oct. 1, 1946, p. 9.
"Frank's Two Store Sites Sold Here," *Burlington Daily News* [Burlington, VT], Oct 01, 1945, p. 6.
"Franks Economy Store, North St. Is Sold to Two Schenectady Men," *The Burlington Free Press* [Burlington, VT], Jun. 28, 1945, p. 9.
Stock Issue, *Albans Daily Messenger*, [Montpelier, VT], Oct. 08, 1945, p. 7.

Property Owned References

Bus Depot
"Railway to Remove Trolleys From Fuller Street Barns," *The Schenectady Gazette,* [Schenectady, NY], Oct. 6, 1931, p.2.
"Auction of Railway Company Assets to Resume Today," *The Schenectady Gazette*, [Schenectady, NY], Sept. 10, 1952, s.2, p.1.
"$500,000 Bid For Dorp Bus Property," *The Times Record*, [Troy, N Y], Sept. 9, 1952, p.17.
"Sch'dy Bus Co. Gets High Bids," *Albany Times Union*, [Albany, NY], Sept. 10, 1952, p.17.
"Schenectady Bus Bids Near $700,000 Mark," *The Times Record*, [Troy, N Y], Sept. 10, 1952, p.15.
"Confirms Sale of Schenectady Bus Property," *Amsterdam Evening Recorder*, [Amsterdam, NY], Sept. 11, 1952, p.2.
"Schenectady Bus Line Franchise Sought by Canadian Firms at Sale," *Knickerbocker News*, [Albany, NY], Sept. 9, 1952, p. (unknown).
"2 Canadians Bid in Dorp Bus Franchise," *The Morning Herald*, [Gloversville and Johnstown, NY], Sept. 11, 1952, p.1.
"City Pushing Bus Terminal Development," *The Schenectady Gazette,* [Schenectady, NY], Apr. 16, 1954, s.2, p.1.
"City Gets Plans for Erie Blvd. Bus Depot," *The Schenectady Gazette,* [Schenectady, NY], May 20, 1954.
"Qualification For Bus Depot Is Attacked," May 26, 1954, *The Schenectady Gazette,* [Schenectady, NY], s.2, p.1.
"City Pushing Bus Terminal Development," *The Schenectady Gazette*, [Schenectady, NY], 1954, s.2, p.1.
"Bus Depot Proposal Is Advanced," *The Schenectady Gazette*, [Schenectady, NY], June 11, 1954, s.2, p.1.
"Streetcar Barn Owner Seeks Clear Title," *The Schenectady Gazette*, [Schenectady, NY], June 16, 1954, s.2, p.1.
"Canadians Lease Bus Terminal," *The Schenectady Gazette*, [Schenectady, NY], Sept. 23, 1952, s.2, p.1.
"Canadian, Seeking To Run Local Bus Lines, Says He Would Operate All Old Routes," *The Schenectady Gazette*, [Schenectady, NY], Apr. 29, 1953, s.2, p.1.
"Union Buys Old Car Barn," *The Schenectady Gazette*, [Schenectady, NY], June 2, 1956.

Emmons/Delta House
"Court Must Decide If College Fraternity Constitutes A Family," *The Schenectady Gazette*, [Schenectady, NY], Apr. 16, 1948, s.2, p.1.
"City, Fraternity in Legal Row Over This House," *The Schenectady Gazette*, [Schenectady, NY], Apr. 17, 1948, s2, p.1.
"Fraternity Served With Order," *The Schenectady Gazette*, [Schenectady, NY], Apr. 17, 1948, s.2, p.1.
"Delta Chi Ouster Hits Legal Snag," *The Schenectady Gazette*, [Schenectady, NY], Apr. 30, 1948, s.2, p.1.
"Delta Chi Case Postponed Week," *The Concordiensis*, Union College, [Schenectady, NY], Apr. 30, 1948.
"Fraternity City Attys. To Parley," *The Schenectady Gazette*, [Schenectady, NY], May 6, 1948, s.2, p.1.
"D-Chi Ouster Move Delayed," *The Concordiensis*, Union College, [Schenectady, NY], May 7, 1948, p. 3.
"Fraternity Hits Zoning Ordinance," *The Schenectady Gazette*, [Schenectady, NY], May 12, 1948, s.2, p.1.
"Attorneys for City, Fraternity Confer In Effort to Reach Agreement on Facts," *The Schenectady Gazette*, [Schenectady, NY], May 21, 1948, p.10.
"76 Actions Filed to Cut Assessments," *The Schenectady Gazette*, [Schenectady, NY], Oct. 11, 1950, p.32.
"Alco Leads in Appeal For Assessment Cuts," *The Schenectady Gazette*, [Schenectady, NY], Oct. 10, 1952.
"City Renews 'Row' With Fraternities," *The Schenectady Gazette*, [Schenectady, NY], Nov. 7 1952, s.2, p1.
"Court Battle Between City, Fraternity, Not Over Yet," *The Schenectady Gazette*, [Schenectady, NY], June 11, 1953 s.2, p.1.
"City Claims Fraternity's Appeal Invalid," *The Schenectady Gazette*, [Schenectady, NY], Apr. 29, 1964, s.2, p.1.
"First Unitarian Society to Purchase Fraternity Site," *The Schenectady Gazette*, [Schenectady, NY], Oct. 29, 1956.
"On Wendell Avenue," (photo) *The Schenectady Gazette*, [Schenectady, NY], Oct. 29, 1956.
"City Demands Union Fraternities Vacate 'GE Realty Plot' Homes," *The Schenectady Gazette*, [Schenectady, NY], Feb. 19, 1959, p.18.
Property Record, First Unitarian Society of Schenectady, 1227 Wendell Ave. [Schenectady, NY].
"Zoning Issue Unresolved: Mrs. Trench," *The Schenectady Gazette*, [Schenectady, NY], Feb. 1, 1957, p.16.
State of New York Supreme Court of the, Appellate Division, Third Judicial Department, City of Schenectady, NY, Plaintiff-Respondent Joseph Grosberg, Samuel Scheinzeit, against Alumni Association of Union Chapter, Delta Chi Fraternity, Inc., Defendants-Appellants, pp. 1-50.

Grosberg Building, Erie Blvd. 138 140 142

"Name Referees In Assessment Controversies," 140 Erie Blvd., *The Schenectady Gazette*, [Schenectady, NY], Oct. 1, 1930, p.9.

Newspaper Notice of Building Permit (Alteration for 140-142 Erie Blvd), *The Schenectady Gazette*, [Schenectady, NY], Jan. 16, 1931, p.6.

"Roller Skating Rink Will Open Here Thursday," *The Schenectady Gazette*, [Schenectady, NY], Jan. 14, 1931, p.5.

Newspaper Ad, Palace Roller Rink, *The Schenectady Gazette*, [Schenectady, NY], Jan. 31, 1931, p.(unknown).

Display Ad, Barron-Burtiss, Inc. located in the new Grosberg Building, *The Schenectady Gazette*, [Schenectady, NY], Feb. 28, 1931, p.(unknown).

Display Ad, Barron-Burtiss, Inc. located in the new Grosberg Building, *The Schenectady Gazette*, [Schenectady, NY], March 7, 1931, p.(unknown).

Display Ad, Large Store To Let on Erie Blvd, *The Schenectady Gazette*, [Schenectady, NY], May 15, 1931, p.40.

Newspaper Ad, Dancing at Silver Slipper, *The Schenectady Gazette*, [Schenectady, NY], Oct. 9, 1931, p.6.

Classified Ad, Refreshment Concession Lease in Silver Slipper, *The Schenectady Gazette*, [Schenectady, NY], Sept. 25 1931, p.(unknown).

Newspaper Ad, Silver Slipper Ballroom, *The Schenectady Gazette*, [Schenectady, NY], Nov. 26, 1931, p.22.

Newspaper Ads (2), Silver Slipper Ballroom, *The Schenectady Gazette*, [Schenectady, NY], Jan. 9, 1932, p.22.

Newspaper Ad, Dance at Silver Slipper, *The Schenectady Gazette*, [Schenectady, NY], Jan. 11, 1932, p.20.

Newspaper Ad, To Let Silver Slipper Ballroom, *The Schenectady Gazette*, [Schenectady, NY], Feb. 12 & 15, 1932, p.32.

Newspaper Ad, Palace Roller Rink, *The Schenectady Gazette*, [Schenectady, NY], Oct. 2, 1933, p.7.

Newspaper Ad, Palace Roller Rink, *The Schenectady Gazette*, [Schenectady, NY], Dec 23, 1935, p.24.

Newspaper Ad, Palace Roller Rink, *The Schenectady Gazette*, [Schenectady, NY], Nov. 3, 1937, p.14.

Newspaper Ad, Palace Roller Rink, *The Schenectady Gazette*, [Schenectady, NY], Oct. 28, 1938, p.16.

"Named Organist for Roller Skating Rink," *The Schenectady Gazette*, [Schenectady, NY], Sept. 30, 1938.

Newspaper Ad, Palace Roller Rink, *The Schenectady Gazette*, [Schenectady, NY], Feb. 18, 1939, p.8.

Newspaper Ad, Palace Roller Rink, *The Schenectady Gazette*, [Schenectady, NY], Nov. 6, 1942, p.21.

"Carl Liss Co. Buys Grosberg Building," *The Schenectady Gazette*, [Schenectady, NY], Jan. 16, 1963, s.2p.17.

"Vintage Diner is 'Wheeled Out,'" *The Schenectady Gazette*, [Schenectady, NY], Sept. 8, 1964, p.17.

"Diner at 140 Erie Blvd. Not One of the 'All Nighters'," *The Schenectady Gazette*, [Schenectady, NY], Sept. 9, 1964, p.19.

Hart, Larry "Remembering City Retailer C.S. Smith," *The Sunday Gazette,* [Schenectady, NY], June 20, 1999, p. B7.

Bump, Bethany, "Historic Schenectady Warehouse to be Overhauled," *The Daily Gazette*, [Schenectady, NY], Aug. 18, 2014. https://dailygazette.com/article/2014/08/18/0818warehouse

Imperial Building Owned With Abe Cohen

"Baum's Newsroom Will be Near Present Site," *The Schenectady Gazette*, [Schenectady, NY], May 21, 1920, p.10.

"Cohen and Grosberg to Remodel Building," *The Schenectady Gazette*, [Schenectady, NY], May 9, 1927.

"Modern $125,00 Building Being Built at State and Center Sts.," *The Schenectady Gazette*, [Schenectady, NY], May 19, 1927, p.(unknown).

Classified Ad, Mentioning the Cohen-Grosberg Building near S. Center Road, *The Schenectady Gazette*, [Schenectady, NY], June 14, 1927, p.(unknown).

"8 More Ask a Reduction in Assessment," *The Schenectady Gazette*, [Schenectady, NY], Sept. 23, 1932.

"Referees in Assessment Suits Named," *The Schenectady Gazette*, [Schenectady, NY], Oct. 8, 1932, p.15.

"Set Dates for Hearings on Assessments," *The Schenectady Gazette*, [Schenectady, NY], Oct. 19, 1932.

Newspaper Notice, Building Permit, 333 State Street, *The Schenectady Gazette*, [Schenectady, NY], Mar. 23, 1939, p.10.

"Child Unhurt When Tiles Fall Three Stories Into Pram," *The Schenectady Gazette*, [Schenectady, NY], Mar. 1, 1946

"Mr. Cohen to Address Unit at Center," *The Schenectady Gazette*, [Schenectady, NY], Oct. 1, 1955, p.11.

"Abe Cohen, Imperial Owner, Stays Young With Styles," *The Schenectady Gazette*, [Schenectady, NY], Oct. 25, 1962.

"Funeral Services Held for Abe Cohen," *The Schenectady Gazette*, [Schenectady, NY], Dec. 19, 1964, p.17.

"Historic Lorraine Block, Symbol of City's Prosperity Falls Victim of Progress," *The Schenectady Gazette*, [Schenectady, NY], June 24, 1972, p.17.

Buell, Bill, "LANDMARKS: Old Imperial Site In Downtown Schenectady Enters A New Phase With Mexican Radio On The Horizon," Life & Arts *The Schenectady Gazette*, [Schenectady, NY], Oct. 27, 2013.

47 Van Guysling

Classified Ad, To Let, Van Guysling Warehouse, *The Schenectady Gazette*, [Schenectady, NY], Mar. 3, 1923, p.18.

Classified Ad, To Let, Brick Warehouse, *The Schenectady Gazette*, [Schenectady, NY], Jan. 30, 1925, p.22.

Classified Ad, To Let, Brick Building, Garage, & Sheds, *The Schenectady Gazette*, [Schenectady, NY], Feb. 18, 1925, p.5.

Classified Ad, To Let, Brick Building, *The Schenectady Gazette*, [Schenectady, NY], Feb. 24, 1925, p.18.

Classified Ad, To Let, Van Guysling Warehouse, *The Schenectady Gazette*, [Schenectady, NY], Mar. 28, 1930, p.39.

Classified Ad, To Let, Van Guysling Warehouse, *The Schenectady Gazette*, [Schenectady, NY], Apr. 3, 1930, p.27.
Classified Ad, To Let, Warehouse on Van Guysling Ave." *The Schenectady Gazette*, [Schenectady, NY], May 15, 1931
Classified Ad, To Let, Van Guysling Warehouse, *The Schenectady Gazette*, [Schenectady, NY], May 18, 1930, p.23.
Display Ad, To Let Van Guysling Warehouse, *The Schenectady Gazette*, [Schenectady, NY], May (date unknown), 1934 p. (unknown).
Newspaper Notice, Real Estate Transfer (47 Van Guysling Ave from Rae Grosberg to Samuel Garbowitz), *The Schenectady Gazette*, [Schenectady, NY], Dec. 19, 1935, p6.
"Van Guysling Avenue Warehouse the Scene of a $15,000 Blaze," *The Schenectady Gazette,* [Schenectady, NY], Jan. 18, 1937, p. 1.
Classified Ad, To Let Warehouse, *The Schenectady Gazette*, [Schenectady, NY], May 20, 1934.
"$15,000 Blaze in Schenectady," *The Saratogian*, [Saratoga Springs, NY], Jan. 18, 1937.
"Warehouse Fire at Schenectady with $15,000 Damage," *Ballston Spa Daily Journal*, [Ballston, NY], Jan. 18, 1937, p.2.
Newspaper Notice, Building Permit (for Samuel Garbowitz, 47-49 Van Guysling), *The Schenectady Gazette,* [Schenectady, NY], Feb. 11, 1937, p.6.

Miscellaneous

Water and Sewer Assessment (South Centre Street-Anna Grosberg), Journal of the Common Council 1901-1902.
Water and Sewer Assessment (Crane Street-Jacob Grosberg), Proceedings of The Common Council City Of Schenectady, Feb. 11, 1908.
Water and Sewer Assessment (Crane Street-Jacob Grosberg), Proceedings of The Common Council City Of Schenectady, Nov. 23, 1909, p.402.
Water and Sewer Assessment (Crane Street-Jacob Grosberg), Proceedings of The Common Council City Of Schenectady, Dec. 15, 1909.
"Real Estate Sales," Jacob and Anna Grosberg to Joseph Grosberg, Lot 25, Hattie Place, *The Schenectady Gazette*, [Schenectady, NY], Nov. 28, 1911, p.6.
"Real Estate Sales," Jacob Grosberg and Anna to Ralph Jeffee, Crane Street, *The Schenectady Gazette*, [Schenectady, NY], Apr. 3, 1913.
"Real Estate Sales," Joseph and Rae Grosberg, Hattie Place, *The Schenectady Gazette*, [Schenectady, NY], Aug 5, 1913, p. 5.
"Real Estate Sales," Jacob Grosberg & Son, Glenville, Lot 51, Crestline Park, *The Schenectady Gazette*, [Schenectady, NY], Oct. 5, 1914, p.5.
"Real Estate Sales," Jacob Grosberg and wife to Joseph Grosberg, Van Guysling Avenue Lot and S. Center Street, *The Schenectady Gazette*, [Schenectady, NY], Apr. 22, 1915.
"Report of County Auditor," *The Schenectady Gazette*, [Schenectady, NY], Sept. 4, 1923.
Real Estate Notice, House on Union Street, *The Schenectady Gazette*, [Schenectady, NY], Apr. 16, 1924, p.8.
Classified Ad, To Let Erie Blvd, *The Schenectady Gazette*, [Schenectady, NY], June 4, 1925.
Classified Ad, To Let, Warehouse, *The Schenectady Gazette*, [Schenectady, NY], Apr. 8, 1925.
Classified Ad, Floor Space to Rent, *Amsterdam Evening Recorder*, [Amsterdam, NY], Nov. 6, 13, 20, 23, 25, 1925.
"Council Not Expected to Provide More Money for Paving Repairs; Hamilton Street Widening Request Unlikely to Get Consideration," *The Schenectady Gazette*, [Schenectady, NY], July 4, 1927, p. (unknown).
"Residents Meet to Discuss Extension of Hamilton Street," *The Schenectady Gazette*, [Schenectady, NY], Sept 24, 1927, p.(unknown).
Newspaper Notice, Building Permit, Alteration to Garage, 110 Erie Blvd., *The Schenectady Gazette*, [Schenectady, NY], Feb. 20, 1929.
Classified Ad, To Let, Large Loft On Erie Blvd., *The Schenectady Gazette*, [Schenectady, NY], Sept. 9, 1929.
Newspaper Notice, Building Permit, brick store, 271 Erie Blvd, *The Schenectady Gazette*, [Schenectady, NY], Apr. 8, 1930, p.4.
Real Estate Transfer Notice, 271-73 Erie Blvd, *The Schenectady Gazette*, [Schenectady, NY], July 2, 1930, p.15.
Classified Ad, To Let, Floor space on Erie Blvd and building on Van Guysling Ave., *The Schenectady Gazette*, [Schenectady, NY], Aug. 8, 1930, p.30.
Classified Ad, To Let, Floor space on Erie Blvd and Van Guysling 3 story building, *The Schenectady Gazette*, [Schenectady, NY], August 11, 1930, p.16.
"Judge Sawyer to Hear Salvation Army Case; FitzJames, Grosberg, and Kresge Disputes," *The Schenectady Gazette*, [Schenectady, NY], Oct. 1, 1930, p.9.
Real Estate Notice, (Mayer Cramer and Joseph Grosberg purchase 1000, 1002, & 1004 State Street), *The Schenectady Gazette*, [Schenectady, NY], Oct. 11, 1930, p.13.
Newspaper Notice, Building Permit, brick gas station on State and Swan Street, *The Schenectady Gazette*, [Schenectady, NY], Apr. 11, 1931, p.8.
"Wide Variance In Valuations," *The Schenectady Gazette*, [Schenectady, NY], Feb. 18, 1933, p.5.
Real Estate Notice, (Joseph Grosberg transfers 1000, 1002, & 1004 State Street to Mayer Cramer), *The Schenectady Gazette*, [Schenectady, NY], June 5, 1937, p.5.

Jewish Affairs References

Aqudat Achim
"Scroll of The Law Is Presented at Synagogue," *The Schenectady Gazette*, [Schenectady, NY], June 4, 1923, p.3.
"Jewish Youth's Future To Be Grosberg's Topic," *The Schenectady Gazette*, [Schenectady, NY], Feb. 13, 1925, p.8.
Skoburn, Henry, *The Agudat Achim Chronicle*, "Commemorating 120 years 1892–2012 Congregation Agudat Achim; 120 years of commitment to Conservative Judaism."
Funeral Notice for Brother Morris, *The Schenectady Gazette*, [Schenectady, NY], Feb. 16, 1929 p.22.
Funeral Notice for Sister Naomi Gold, *The Schenectady Gazette*, [Schenectady, NY], Feb. 19, 1929, p.7.
"25-Year Club of Synagogue Honor Guests," *The Schenectady Gazette*, [Schenectady, NY], May 26, 1931, p.21.
The Bulletin, Official Organ of Congregation Agudath Achim, [Schenectady, NY], Vol. 1, Sept. 1931.
"Dr. Abrams To Be Installed By Synagogue," *The Schenectady Gazette*, [Schenectady, NY], Nov. 14, 1931, p. 9.
The Bulletin, Official Organ of Congregation Agudath Achim, [Schenectady, NY], Nov. 1931.
"Mrs. Wallach Elected Head of Sisterhood," *The Schenectady Gazette*, [Schenectady, NY], June 9, 1932, p.8.
"Sisterhood Holds Festive Meeting," *The Schenectady Gazette*, [Schenectady, NY], Oct. 19, 1932.
"Congregation Names Board," *The Schenectady Gazette*, [Schenectady, NY], Nov. 4, 1932, p.8.
"Region United Synagogue to Convene Here," *The Schenectady Gazette*, [Schenectady, NY], Jan.20, 1933, p. (unknown).
"Terrace Sisterhood to Hold Card Party," *The Schenectady Gazette*, [Schenectady, NY], Apr. 25, 1934, p.12.
"Synagogue to Seat Officers Sunday Night," *The Schenectady Gazette*, [Schenectady, NY], 1934.
"Sisterhood at Nott Terrace Installs Staff," *The Schenectady Gazette*, [Schenectady, NY], 1934.
"Synagogue Will Hear Grosberg," *The Schenectady Gazette*, [Schenectady, NY], Apr. 11, 1935, p.7.
"Terrace Synagogue Sisterhood Bazaar to Be Opened Tomorrow," *The Schenectady Gazette*, [Schenectady, NY], Nov. 30, 1935, p.9.
"Purpose of Young Judea to Be Told at Event Tonight," *The Schenectady Gazette*, [Schenectady, NY], Jan. 10, 1936.
"Terrace Synagogue Sisterhood Arranges Drama, Card Party," *The Schenectady Gazette*, [Schenectady, NY], Jan. 8, 1936, p.13.
"Complete Plans to Rededicate Synagogue," *The Schenectady Gazette*, [Schenectady, NY], June 7, 1941, p.10.
"First U.S. Envoy to Israel Will Speak Here Monday," *The Schenectady Gazette*, [Schenectady, NY], June 6, 1953, S2, p.1.
"Agudas Achim to Install 24 Trustees Tomorrow," *The Schenectady Gazette*, [Schenectady, NY], June 5, 1958, p.25.
"Local Committee, State of Israel Bonds, Schedules Fashion-Festival Dinner, May 20," *The Schenectady Gazette*, [Schenectady, NY], May 15, 1959, p.26.
"9 Agudat Achim Past Leaders to Be Cited," *The Schenectady Gazette*, [Schenectady, NY], Sept. 24, 1964, p.14.
"Agudat Achim," Schenectady County Historical Society, https://schenectadyhist.wordpress.com/2010/01/ Jan. 7, 2010.

B'nai B'rith
"B'nai B'rith To Seat Staff, "*The Schenectady Gazette*, [Schenectady, NY], Apr. 10, 1940, p.7.
"Heads B'nai B'rith," *The Schenectady Gazette*, [Schenectady, NY], Apr. 12, 1940, p.13.
"B'nai B'rith to Welcome Rabbi Miller, *The Schenectady Gazette*, [Schenectady, NY], May 22, 1940, p.3.
"B'nai B'rith Will Hear Dr.Mashioff," *The Schenectady Gazette*, [Schenectady, NY], Apr. 11, 1944, p.24.
"2 Committees of B'nai B'rith Club Named," *The Schenectady Gazette*, [Schenectady, NY], date (unknown) 1954, p. (unknown).
"B'nai B'rith Service Club to Fight Sale Of Salacious Material," *The Schenectady Gazette*, [Schenectady, NY], Oct. 19, 1954, p.2.
"National Units Study Success of B'nai B'rith," *The Schenectady Gazette*, [Schenectady, NY], Dec. 3, 1954, p.2.
"B'nai B'rith Picks Graubart Chairman of Service Unit," *The Schenectady Gazette*, [Schenectady, NY], date (unknown) 1954, p. (unknown).
"3 Chairmen of Jewish Groups Named," *The Schenectady Gazette*, [Schenectady, NY], date (unknown) 1954, p.(unknown).

Bonds for Israel
"Mayor Hushi Will Launch Israel Bond Issue Today," *The Schenectady Gazette*, [Schenectady, NY], June 5, 1952, p.9.
"Abe Cohen Heads 'Bonds For Israel'," *The Schenectady Gazette*, [Schenectady, NY], May 27, 1955, p. (unknown).
"To Talk Here for Israel Bond Drive," *The Schenectady Gazette*, [Schenectady, NY], June 7, 1956, p.20.
"Cramer Named Chairman of Israeli Bond Drive," *The Schenectady Gazette*, [Schenectady, NY], June 5, 1958, p.7.
"Israel Bond Supper Set at Van Curler," *The Schenectady Gazette*, [Schenectady, NY], June 11, 1958, p.10.
"Israel Official To Speak for Bond Drive," *The Schenectady Gazette*, [Schenectady, NY], June 13, 1958 p.12.
"Israeli Military Hero to Speak at Supper," *The Schenectady Gazette*, [Schenectady, NY], June 30, 1958, p. (unknown).
"Committee to Aid in Israel Bond Drive Is Announced," *The Schenectady Gazette*, [Schenectady, NY], Apr. 21, 1959, p.12.
"Israeli Intelligence Aide To Address Bond Dinner," *The Schenectady Gazette*, [Schenectady, NY], May 6, 1960, p.5.

Hadassah Women's Zionist

"Chanukah to Sponsor Program of Cultural Work During Winter" *The Schenectady Gazette*, [Schenectady, NY], Dec. 13, 1926, p. 15.

"Hadassah Celebrates Seventh Anniversary by Saratoga Dinner," *The Schenectady Gazette*, [Schenectady, NY], June 22, 1928, p. (unknown).

"Hadassah Completes All Arrangements for Election Night Dance," *The Schenectady Gazette*, [Schenectady, NY], Oct. 26, 1928, p.5.

"Senior Hadassah to Hold Card Party Next Sunday Night," *The Schenectady Gazette*, [Schenectady, NY], Dec. 17, 1929, p.11.

"Officers Named by Hadassah Chapter," *The Schenectady Gazette*, [Schenectady, NY], May 10. 1930, p.18.

"Cowen to Be Speaker At Zionist Meeting," *The Schenectady Gazette*, [Schenectady, NY], October 30, 1926, p.(unknown).

"Hadassah Plans Several Activities, *The Schenectady Gazette*, [Schenectady, NY], Apr. 21, 1931, p 20.

"Plans Complete For Luncheon Of Hadassah," *The Schenectady Gazette*, [Schenectady, NY], June 8, 1931, p.10.

"Senior Hadassah To Meet Tonight," *The Schenectady Gazette*, [Schenectady, NY], Apr. 11, 1932, p. (unknown).

"Jewish Home Is Described To Hadassah," *The Schenectady Gazette*, [Schenectady, NY], Nov. 17, 1932, p.5.

"Mrs. Peltman and Mrs. Grosberg At Hadassah Meet," *The Schenectady Gazette*, [Schenectady, NY], Sept. 20, 1932, p.2.

"To Exhibit 30 Reiss Paintings," *The Schenectady Gazette*, [Schenectady, NY], May 14, 1935, p. (unknown).

"Music and Tea for Hadassah," *The Schenectady Gazette*, [Schenectady, NY], date (unknown) 1935, p. (unknown).

"Sr. Hadassah Conference Next Week," *Times-Union*, [Albany, NY], May 8, 1938, p.4-C.

"Women to Hear Hadassah Head," *The Schenectady Gazette*, [Schenectady, NY], June 4, 1938, p.15.

"President of Hadassah Reveals New Projects," *The Schenectady Gazette*, [Schenectady, NY], Sept. 1, 1938, p.17

"Schenectady Chapter, Sr. Hadassah, Elects Executive Board," *The Schenectady Gazette*, [Schenectady, NY], Apr. 17, 1940, p.17.

"Will Discuss Jewish Music," *The Schenectady Gazette*, [Schenectady, NY], Oct. 15, 1940, p.14.

"Mrs. Lurie Reports on Convention," *The Schenectady Gazette*, [Schenectady, NY], Nov. 8, 1940, p.32.

"Mrs. Paul Entertain," *Albany Times-Union* [Albany, NY], Dec. 6, 1940, p.19.

"Announce Reservations for Senior Hadassah Luncheon," *The Schenectady Gazette*, [Schenectady, NY], May 20, 1941, p.11.

"Mrs. Jay Breslaw Installed as Head of Senior Hadassah," *The Schenectady Gazette*, [Schenectady, NY], May 21, 1941, p. 13.

"Hadassah to Have Oct. Fashion Show," *The Schenectady Gazette*, [Schenectady, NY], Sept. 10, 1941, p.15.

"List Sahr Recital Subscribers," *The Schenectady Gazette*, [Schenectady, NY], Nov. 17, 1942, p.14.

"Local Committee, State of Israel Bonds, Schedules Fashion-Festival Dinner May 20," *The Schenectady Gazette*, [Schenectady, NY], May 15, l959, p.26.

Hebrew Institute

"Jews to Dedicate School Building," *The Schenectady Gazette*, [Schenectady, NY], Dec. 27, 1912, p.7.

"Hebrew Organizations Install New Officers," *The Schenectady Gazette*, [Schenectady, NY], Feb. 5, 1914, p.1.

Listing for Schenectady Hebrew School, *State of New York 10th Annual Report of the Education Department*, The University of the State of New York, March 16, 1914, Volume 42, p.236.

"Plans Are Made For Big Jewish Fair in January," *The Schenectady Gazette*, [Schenectady, NY], Oct. 24, 1914, p.2.

"Local Hebrew Institute to Have Fair January 17," *The Schenectady Gazette*, [Schenectady, NY], Nov. 23, 1914, p.6.

"Hebrew Institute to Hold Bazaar Jan. 17," *The Schenectady Gazette*, [Schenectady, NY], Dec 28, 1914, p.10.

"Local Hebrews Favor Palestine as Race Home," *The Schenectady Gazette*, [Schenectady, NY], Sept. 29, 1915, p.3.

"Jewish Relief Committee Reports Much Progress," *The Schenectady Gazette*, [Schenectady, NY], Jan. 11, 1915, p.10.

"Hebrew Fair's Plans Complete," *The Schenectady Gazette*, [Schenectady, NY], Jan. 11, 1915, p.3.

"Hebrew Fair Will Be Opened Tonight," *The Schenectady Gazette*, [Schenectady, NY], Jan. 18, 1915, p.2.

"Plans Complete for Hebrew Fair," *The Schenectady Gazette*, [Schenectady, NY], Jan. 15, 1915, p.9.

"Expect Big Crowd at Hebrew Fair Tonight," *The Schenectady Gazette*, [Schenectady, NY], Jan. 23, 1915, p.9.

"Hebrew Institute Meeting Monday," *The Schenectady Gazette*, [Schenectady, NY], July 8, 1916, p.2.

"Hebrew Institute To Remain Closed While Paralysis Continues," *The Schenectady Gazette*, [Schenectady, NY], Aug. 24, 1916, p.5.

Schenectady Hebrew School Listing, *Organizations and Institutions*, The University of the State of New York, Oct. 1922, p.144.

"Schenectady Hebrew Institute Building Located on Albany Street" *The Schenectady Gazette*, [Schenectady, NY], Jan. 19, 1924, p.12.

Jewish Appeal

"Celebrate Opening of Big University," *The Schenectady Gazette*, [Schenectady, NY], Apr. 2, 1925.

"Jewish Campaign Ends With Quota of $30,000 Attained," *The Schenectady Gazette*, [Schenectady, NY], June 7, 1926, p.10.
"Schaffer Chairman of Committee that Will Welcome Kenworthy," *The Schenectady Gazette*, [Schenectady, NY], Jan. 27, 1927.
"Million Jews In Poland Are Seen Starving," *The Schenectady Gazette*, [Schenectady, NY], 1935, date (unknown), p.(unknown).
"J.E. Grosberg Head of 1936 Jewish Appeal," *The Schenectady Gazette*, [Schenectady, NY], Oct. 30, 1935, p. 14.
"Noted Hebrew Leader's Talk to Open Drive," *The Schenectady Gazette*, [Schenectady, NY], 1936, date (unknown).
"Jewish Appeal Begins Nov. 8th," *The Schenectady Gazette*, [Schenectady, NY], Oct. 28, 1936, p.24.
"Sch'dy Funds J Drive," *Times-Union*, [Albany, NY], Nov. 5, 1936, p.14.
"Name Jewish Appeal Aides," (Grosberg is Chairman), *The Schenectady Gazette*, [Schenectady, NY], Nov. 5, 1936, p.2.
"Jewry Opens 10-Day Appeal," *The Schenectady Gazette*, [Schenectady, NY], Nov. 11, 1938, p.14.
"Jewish Appeal Aides to Report," *The Schenectady Gazette*, [Schenectady, NY], Nov. 15, 1938, p. (unknown).
"United Jewish Appeal Obtains $15,000 in City," *The Schenectady Gazette*, [Schenectady, NY], Nov. 18, 1938, p. (unknown).
"United Jewish Appeal," *Times Record,* [Troy, NY], Oct. 16, 1939, p.7.
"Jewry in City Maps Appeal to Aid Refugees," *The Schenectady Gazette*, [Schenectady, NY], Nov. 18, 1939, p.22.
"Jewish Leaders Report at Conference on Polish Relief," Citizen Advertiser, [Auburn, NY] 1940 date (unknown), p.12.
"Grosberg Speaks at Jewish Appeal Drive Supper in Glens Falls," *The Schenectady Gazette*, [Schenectady, NY], 1942 date (unknown).
"4 Local Men Named to National Council on Relief," *The Schenectady Gazette*, [Schenectady, NY], Dec. 26, 1944, p.16.
"Dinner to Honor Civic Leader," *Albany Times Union*, [Albany, NY], June 12, 1958, p.5.
"At UJA Meet in Florida," *The Schenectady Gazette*, [Schenectady, NY], Feb. 17, 1961, p.9.
"Local Jewish Leaders Will Aid Campaign," *The Schenectady Gazette*, [Schenectady, NY], Feb. 27, 1961, p.7.

Jewish Community Center (JCC)

"Schenectady Club Is To Be Dissolved And Building Sold," *The Schenectady Gazette*, [Schenectady, NY], Dec. 3, 1914, p.8.
"United Jewish Charity Drive Begun in City; To Raise $100,000 for Hebrew Community Center to Save Overhead," *The Schenectady Gazette*, [Schenectady, NY], Oct. 11, 1922, p. 2.
"Jewish Community Building to Be Opened Thursday," *The Schenectady Gazette*, [Schenectady, NY], June 11, 1923, p.14.
Newspaper Notice, Building Permits, United Hebrew Community, Germania Ave, *The Schenectady Gazette*, [Schenectady, NY], Oct. 14, 1924, p. (unknown).
"Plans for Jewish Convention Here Now Complete," *The Schenectady Gazette*, [Schenectady, NY], Aug. 31, 1925, p.5.
"Will Dedicate New Jewish Community Building Tomorrow," *The Schenectady Gazette*, [Schenectady, NY], Nov 14, 1925.
"Real Estate at Public Auction," (notice of Germania Ave Turkish Bath House) *The Schenectady Gazette*, [Schenectady, NY], Mar. 21, 1929.
"Sch'dy Jewish Group Will Pick Directors," *Times Union*, [Albany, NY], Apr. 26, 1930, p.2.
"Religious Bath house on Germania Avenue Purchased by Cregan," *The Schenectady Gazette*, [Schenectady, NY], June 7, 1930.
"Union Junior Will Compete At Rochester," *The Schenectady Gazette*, [Schenectady, NY], Oct. 10 1930.
"Jewry to Plan Annual Drive For Members," *The Schenectady Gazette*, [Schenectady, NY], Oct. 14, 1931, p.2.
"To Start Work on Addition to Jewish Center," *The Schenectady Gazette*, [Schenectady, NY], Oct. 28, 1932, p.2.
"Jewish Center Makes Plans for Poverty Dinner, "*The Schenectady Gazette*, [Schenectady, NY], Nov. 25, 1931, p.10.
"Break Ground for Addition to Jewish Center," *The Schenectady Gazette*, [Schenectady, NY], Nov. 1, 1932, p.2.
"Jews to Hold Celebration," *The Schenectady Gazette*, [Schenectady, NY], Nov. 1, 1932, p.14.
"Bookstein to Speak Before Local Jewry," *The Schenectady Gazette*, [Schenectady, NY], Dec. 1, 1932, p.28.
"Cornerstone of Center Is Laid," *The Schenectady Gazette*, [Schenectady, NY], Dec. 5, 1932, p. 2.
"To Dedicate Jewish Center," *The Saratogian*, [Saratoga Springs, NY], Apr. 21, 1933, p.14.
"New Sch'dy Jewish Center Dedicated," *Times-Union*, [Albany, NY], Apr. 24, 1933, p.3
"To Consider Aid for German Jews," *The Schenectady Gazette*, [Schenectady, NY], Sept. 4, 1933, p.12.
"Jewish Center Holds Election," *The Schenectady Gazette*, [Schenectady, NY], 1934 date (unknown).
"Better Citizen Aim of Center Says Coplon," *The Schenectady Gazette*, [Schenectady, NY], May 4, 1936.
"Dinner to Open Jewish Center Jubilee Events," *The Schenectady Gazette*, [Schenectady, NY], Jan. 16, 1937, p.3.
"Friedman Will Talk at Jewish Center Meeting," *The Schenectady Gazette*, [Schenectady, NY], Apr. 29, 1937, p.28.
"Old timers at Jewish Center To Win Praise," *The Schenectady Gazette*, [Schenectady, NY], Jan 14, 1937.
"Center Hub of Hebrew Life," *The Schenectady Gazette*, [Schenectady, NY], Apr. 22, 1938, p.9.
"Jewish Camp Dedication Set," *The Schenectady Gazette*, [Schenectady, NY], June 4, 1938, p.11.
"Entertainment Festival Patron List Announced," *The Schenectady Gazette*, [Schenectady, NY], Nov. 14, 1939.

"Bidders Offer $8,490 in City Tax Lien Sale," *The Schenectady Gazette*, [Schenectady, NY], Aug. 17, 1940.
"Jewish Center To Construct Addition," *The Schenectady Gazette*, [Schenectady, NY], May 1, 1941, p.22.
"Center Women Greet New Members," *The Schenectady Gazette*, [Schenectady, NY], Sept. 29, 1941, p.15.
"Community Center to Fete J. E. Grosberg," *The Schenectady Gazette*, [Schenectady, NY], Nov. 20, 1943.
"Fete Grosberg At Testimonial Dinner At Hotel", *The Schenectady Gazette*, [Schenectady, NY], Nov. 29, 1943, p.9.
"Community Center Elects Tomorrow," *The Schenectady Gazette*, [Schenectady, NY], May 1, 1944, p.3.
"Jewish Community Center to Dedicate New Building," *The Schenectady Gazette*, [Schenectady, NY], June 21, 1944, p.9.
"Hebrew School Will Start Oct. 16," *The Schenectady Gazette*, [Schenectady, NY], Sept. 30, 1944, p.9.
"L.L. Starkman, Jewish Leader, Dies at 75," *The Schenectady Gazette*, [Schenectady, NY], June 8, 1946, s2p1.
"Jewish Unit to Announce New Post," *The Schenectady Gazette*, [Schenectady, NY], May 24, 1952, p.4.
"Hershkowitz Re-Elected by Jewish Center," *The Schenectady Gazette*, [Schenectady, NY], date (unknown) 1955, p.(unknown).
Schenectady Jewish Community Center Board of Directors, Minutes of Board Meeting, Sept 3, 1957.
"Releases Deed," (photo) *The Schenectady Gazette*, [Schenectady, NY], Nov. 5, 1957, p.12.
"Joseph E. Grosberg Releases Deed to Jewish Community Center" *The Schenectady Gazette*, [Schenectady, NY], Nov. 5, 1957
"Gershovitz Will Speak at JCC 46th Annual Meeting," *The Schenectady Gazette*, [Schenectady, NY], June 3, 1958, p.13.
"Weingarten Resigns Jewish Council, Center Directorship for Graduate Studies," *The Schenectady Gazette*, [Schenectady, NY], July 17, 1959.
"J.E. Grosberg Re-elected at Jewish Center," *The Schenectady Gazette*, [Schenectady, NY], Nov. 7, 1960, p.38.
"Gross Elected To Jewish Center Post," *The Schenectady Gazette*, [Schenectady, NY], Nov. 27, 1961, p.30.

Jewish Congress 1916-1917

"Reorganize Congress Committee," *The American Jewish Chronicle*, July 14, 1916, p. 319.
"Nominating Convention Chooses Candidates," *The American Jewish Chronicle*, Vol 3 No. 1-26, May 11, 1917, p. 63.
"Zionists Elect Delegates," *The American Jewish Chronicle*, Vol 3 No. 1-26, May 11, 1917, p. 223.
"Jewish Campaign for Congress To Start Tonight," *The Schenectady Gazette*, [Schenectady, NY], June 6, 1917, p.2.
"Prominent Jewish Speakers Here," *The Morning Herald*, [Gloversville and Johnstown, NY], June 6, 1917, p.8.
"Jews Will Elect Congressman Today," *The Schenectady Gazette*, [Schenectady, NY], June 9, 1917, p.6.
"Rabbi Jasin Congressman by Big Vote," *The Schenectady Gazette*, [Schenectady, NY], June 11, 1917, p.4.
"Zionists Elect," *The Schenectady Gazette*, [Schenectady, NY], Dec. 18, 1918, p.11.
"Rabbi Jasin Is Appointed," *The Morning Herald*, [Gloversville and Johnstown, NY], July 21, 1921, p. 7.
"Seven Candidates Entered in Jewish Congress Elections," *The Schenectady Gazette*, [Schenectady, NY], June 18, 1923, p.14.
"Three Candidates for Jewish Congress Announce Withdrawal," *The Schenectady Gazette*, [Schenectady, NY], June 23, 1923, p.15.

Jewish Home for the Aged/Daughters of Sarah Jewish Home for the Aged

"Hamilton Street Synagogue Re-elects Etkin Fourth Time" (includes appeal for funds for the Jewish Home, Joe Grosberg chairman), *The Schenectady Gazette*, [Schenectady, NY], Sept.4, 1947, p.11.
"Jewish Home," (photo), *The Troy Record*, [Troy, NY], Oct. 26, 1946, p.(unknown).
"Gives Land for Jewish Home for the Aged," *The Schenectady Gazette*, [Schenectady, NY], Sept. 23, 1947, p.2.
"Break Ground For New Jewish Home on Goodman Site," *The Troy Record*, [Troy, NY], Sept. 22, 1947, p.2.
"Jewish Home Cornerstone Rites Slated," *The Schenectady Gazette*, [Schenectady, NY], June 3, 1949, p.12.
"New Jewish Home for Aged At Troy to Open Sunday," *The Schenectady Gazette*, [Schenectady, NY], date (unknown) 1949, p. (unknown).
"Jewish Home," (photo), *The Times Record*, [Troy, NY], Oct. 25, 1949, p.16.
"Officers Elected For Jewish Home," *Times-Union*, [Albany, NY], Mar. 9, 1950, p.10.
"3 From City Installed by Jewish Home," *The Schenectady Gazette*, [Schenectady, NY], Feb. 18, 1953, p.11.
Newspaper notice, Joseph Grosberg of Schenectady was appointed chairman of Capital District Jewish Home For The Aged Executive Committee, *Times-Union*, [Albany, NY], Feb. 24, 1953, p.4.
"Parley on Aged Planned," *The Times Record*, [Troy, NY], Nov. 12, 1953, p.27.
"Jewish Home for Aged Appoints Director's Aide," *Times-Union*, [Albany, NY], Nov. 15, 1953, S-C, p.1.
"Officers of Home Elected," *Knickerbocker News*, [Albany, NY], Feb. 10, 1954.
"Membership Tea for Newly Formed Auxiliary to Jewish Home for the Aged Set Aug. 25," *The Schenectady Gazette*, [Schenectady, NY], Aug. 17, 1954, p.17.
"Jewish Home At Troy Picks New Officers," *Times-Union*, [Albany, NY], May 26, 1955, p.42.
"Attend Picnic," *The Schenectady Gazette*, [Schenectady, NY], Sept. 5, 1957, p. (unknown).
"Jewish Home for the Aged Names 4 Local Men," *The Schenectady Gazette*, [Schenectady, NY], June 11, 1958, p.23.
"Handleman Joins Board of Jewish Home for the Aged," *The Schenectady Gazette*, [Schenectady, NY], 1959. p. 18.
"Jewish Home Cited," *The Times Record*, [Troy, NY], Oct. 16, 1958, p.6.

"Jewish Home Cited," *The Schenectady Gazette*, [Schenectady, NY], Oct. 16, 1958, p.16.
"Jewish Home Elects Yulman President," *Times-Union*, [Albany, NY], May 27, 1961, p.13.
"Jewish Home Sets Election," *The Times Record*, [Troy, NY], May 23, 1968, p.14.
"Jewish Home Unit Meets in Troy Sunday," *The Schenectady Gazette*, [Schenectady, NY], May 23, 1968, p.48.

Jewish Social Service Organization (JSSO)
"Jewish Social Service Organizations Hold Silver Jubilee Dinner," *The Schenectady Gazette*, [Schenectady, NY], May 7, 1938, p.9.
"Jewish Social Service Organization Committees Are Named," *The Schenectady Gazette*, [Schenectady, NY], Sept. 16, 1941, p.13
"Jewish Social Service Women Plan Meeting," *The Schenectady Gazette*, [Schenectady, NY], Oct 19, 1944.
"Social Service Group Honors Mrs. Grosberg," *The Schenectady Gazette*, [Schenectady, NY], Nov. 25, 1943, p.22.
"JSSO Holds Final Meet, Installation," *The Schenectady Gazette*, [Schenectady, NY], June 30, 1945, p.15.
"JSSO to Install Officers on Monday," *The Schenectady Gazette*, [Schenectady, NY], (date unknown) 1949, p.(unknown).
"Installation Set Today," *The Schenectady Gazette*, [Schenectady, NY], May 26, 1952, p.13.
"Installed," (photo) *The Schenectady Gazette*, [Schenectady, NY], May 27, 1954, p.4.
"JSSO Will Mark 41st Anniversary," *The Schenectady Gazette*, [Schenectady, NY], May 17, 1954, p.17.
"JSSO 51st (sic) Installation On Monday," *The Schenectady Gazette*, [Schenectady, NY], May 23, 1954, p.10.
"Grosberg to Speak at JSSO Event," *The Schenectady Gazette*, [Schenectady, NY], date (unknown) 1955, p.(unknown).
"JSSO Fete," (photo of 42 anniversary) *The Schenectady Gazette*, [Schenectady, NY], date (unknown) 1955 p. (unknown).
"JSSO Notes Anniversary With Program," *The Schenectady Gazette*, [Schenectady, NY], June 11, 1957, p.13.
"Jewish Group Will Mark Anniversary," *The Schenectady Gazette*, [Schenectady, NY], May 22, 1958, p.24.
"JSSO Marks Birthday," (photo) *The Schenectady Gazette*, [Schenectady, NY], May 27, 1960, p.22.
"Program Participants," (photo), *Ibid.*
"Organization to Install New Officers," *The Schenectady Gazette*, [Schenectady, NY], May 25, 1963, p.14.
"Installation Scheduled By JSSO," *The Schenectady Gazette*, [Schenectady, NY], May 20, 1967, p.17.
"Mr. Grosberg Will Install New Officers," *The Schenectady Gazette*, [Schenectady, NY], date (unknown) 1968, p.(unknown).

Misc. Jewish Affairs
"Jews To Hold Mass Meeting To Raise Funds," *The Schenectady Gazette*, [Schenectady, NY], Dec. 26, 1914, p.2.
"Jews Urged To See There Are No Future Wars," *The Schenectady Gazette*, [Schenectady, NY], Aug 27, 1917, p.10.
"Much Interest Manifested in Wise Lecture," *The Schenectady Gazette*, [Schenectady, NY], Apr. 25, 1918, p.5.
"Will Raise $35,000 for Jewish Relief," *The Schenectady Gazette*, [Schenectady, NY], Oct. 6, 1919, p.8.
"Jews Will Begin Keren Hayesod Campaign Here at Sunday Mass Meeting," *The Schenectady Gazette*, [Schenectady, NY], Oct. 7, 1921, p.10.
"Orthodox and Reform Jew Unite in Drive for Palestine Fund," *The Schenectady Gazette*, [Schenectady, NY], Feb. 15, 1923, p. 9.
"Call to Jews," *The Schenectady Gazette*, [Schenectady, NY], 1923.
"Will Lecture Here on Palestine Fund," *The Schenectady Gazette*, [Schenectady, NY], May 20, 1925, p.8.
"Rabbi to Speak Here for Appeal In Palestine Aid," *The Schenectady Gazette*, [Schenectady, NY], Dec. 14, 1925.
"Jewish Organizations to Celebrate Chanukah," *The Schenectady Gazette*, [Schenectady, NY], Dec. 4, 1926, p.1
"Fifteen Million Dollars," Letter to David A. Brown, National Chairman United Jewish Campaign from Abraham Ferber, Jan. 25, 1927.
"Rabbi Rosen to Conduct First Service Here Tomorrow Night," *The Schenectady Gazette*, [Schenectady, NY], Sept. 15, 1927, p.(unknown).
"Palestine Fund Appeal Opened At Big Meeting," *Times-Union*, [Albany, NY], Dec. 14, 1927, p.(unknown).
"Local Jews to Raise $7,500 for Palestine Establishment Fund," *The Schenectady Gazette*, [Schenectady, NY], Apr. 9, 1928, p.4.
"Fifteen Million Dollars," Letter to David A. Brown, National Chairman United Jewish Campaign from Abraham Ferber, July 11, 1928.
"Lehman to Address Jews at Emergency Relief Conference," Dec. 3, 1928.
"Palestine Emergency Relief Fund Reaches Total of $2,257.66," *The Schenectady Gazette*, [Schenectady, NY], Sept. 16, 1929, p.5.
"Committee for Tool Campaign to Assist Jews Has Meeting," *The Schenectady Gazette*, [Schenectady, NY], Feb. 1, 1930, p. 19.
"Over 50 Jews Attend Rally," *The Schenectady Gazette*, [Schenectady, NY], Oct. 17, 1930, p.5.
"Jewish Women to Help Curb Unemployment," *The Schenectady Gazette*, [Schenectady, NY], Nov. 26, 1930, p.9.
"Benefit Concert," (for Judea Convalescent Home) *The Schenectady Gazette*, [Schenectady, NY], Aug. 11, 1931, p.8.
"Conference of Jewish Workers," *Amsterdam Evening Recorder*, [Amsterdam, NY], Nov 23, 1931, p.7.
"Jewry Holds Big 'Poverty Dinner' Sunday," *The Schenectady Gazette*, [Schenectady, NY], Nov. 27, 1931, p.6.
"Aid Palestine Fund," *Ballston Spa Daily Journal*, [Ballston, NY], Dec. 1, 1931, p.5.

"United Synagogue Convention Held," *Kingston Daily Freeman*, [Kingston, NY], Jan. 30, 1932, p.5.
"Jewry to End Big Campaign," *The Schenectady Gazette*, [Schenectady, NY], Jan. 12, 1932.
"Rally Planned at Synagogue," *Times-Union*, [Albany, NY], Dec. 4, 1932,2-B.
"District Women Rally Dec 14 for United Synagogue," *The Saratogian*, [Saratoga Springs, NY], Dec. 5, 1932, p.7.
"Jewish Women To Rally Here," *The Schenectady Gazette*, [Schenectady, NY], Dec. 7, 1932.
"Installment For Sherman Held," *The Schenectady Gazette*, [Schenectady, NY], Nov 27, 1933, p.7.
"Fraternal and Other Groups in NRA Parade," *The Schenectady Gazette*, [Schenectady, NY], Sept. 1933, p.3.
"Jewish Women Of Federation Elect Officers," *The Schenectady Gazette*, [Schenectady, NY], Feb. 4, 1935.
"Grosberg to Lecture On Trip to Palestine," *The Schenectady Gazette*, [Schenectady, NY], Apr. 22, 1935, p.2.
"Jews Hold Flower Day Event Tomorrow," (Jewish National Council Fund/Joe Grosberg chairman), *The Schenectady Gazette*, [Schenectady, NY], June 8, 1935, p.(unknown).
"J. E. Grosberg Head of 1936 Jewish Appeal," *The Schenectady Gazette*, [Schenectady, NY], Oct. 30, 1935
"Area Speaking Contest," *The Times-Union*, [Albany, NY], Apr. 29, 1937.
"7 Schenectady Men Listed as Notable Jews," *The Schenectady Gazette*, [Schenectady, NY], Feb. 14, 1938, p.15.
"Grosberg Heads Drive For Jewish Relief Funds," Apr. 19, 1939.
"2 Syracusans Are Named by Jewish Group," *Syracuse Herald-Journal* [Syracuse, NY], Oct. 9, 1939, s.2, p.1.
"Six Will Attend National Meeting," *The Schenectady Gazette*, [Schenectady, NY], Nov. 30, 1939, p.5.
"Jewish Leaders Called To Regional Conference" Citizen Advertiser [Auburn, NY], March (date unknown) 1940, p. (unknown).
"Jewish Leaders Report at Conference on Polish Relief," Citizen Advertiser [Auburn, NY], date (unknown) 1940, p.12.
"Grosberg to Attend Syracuse Conference," *The Schenectady Gazette*, [Schenectady, NY], Mar. 27, 1940.
"500 Jewish Leaders Here, Will Study Problems Due to Persecutions," *Syracuse Journal*, [Syracuse, NY], Mar. 27, 1940, p.12.
"District Jewish Leaders Honored," *Knickerbocker News*, [Albany, NY], Apr. 8, 1940, p. 2-B.
"Jewish Leaders Attend Conference in Syracuse," *Daily Sentinel*, [Rome, NY], Apr. 9, 1940, p.3.
"Exhibit of Jewish Articles Opens at Schenectady Museum," *The Schenectady Gazette*, [Schenectady, NY], May 4, 1940, p.14.
"Outstanding Jewish Figures to Speak Here," *The Schenectady Gazette*, [Schenectady, NY], Oct. 10, 1940, p.11.
"Senior Hadassah Elects Officers for Coming Year; Mrs. Louis Yaguda Is Named President, Committees Selected for Many Projects," *Times Union*, [Albany, NY], May 28, 1941, p.15.
"Senior Hadassah Committees Named By Mrs. Yaguda," *Knickerbocker News*, [Albany, NY], May 22, 1941, p.1B.
"Youth Aliyah Drive to End Thursday," *Knickerbocker News*, [Albany, NY], Dec. 8, 1941, p.B-5.
"To Have Panel on India," *The Schenectady Gazette*, [Schenectady, NY], Dec. 5, 1942, p. (unknown).
"N.C.J.W. To Hear Talk On Russia," *The Schenectady Gazette*, [Schenectady, NY], Nov. 8, 1943.
"Grosberg Presented Plaque," *The Schenectady Gazette*, [Schenectady, NY], Nov. 29, 1943.
"4 Local Men Named to National Council on Jewish Relief," *The Schenectady Gazette*, [Schenectady, NY], Dec. 26, 1944, p. 16.
"Attend Dessert Bridge at Shaker Ridge," *The Schenectady Gazette*, [Schenectady, NY], July 26, 1945, p.17.
"Jewish Council Starts Action to Incorporate, *The Schenectady Gazette*, [Schenectady, NY], Apr. 22, 1948, p.14.
"Mass Meeting Will Hail New Jewish State," *The Schenectady Gazette*, [Schenectady, NY], May 19, 1948, s.2, p.1.
"Jewish People Wil Emerge Victorious, Speaker Tells 'Salute-to-Israel' Meeting," *The Schenectady Gazette*, [Schenectady, NY], May 21, 1948, s2-p.1.
Letter to Dr. Bernhard Kahn, Joint Distribution Committee from Henry Montor, "United Palestine Appeal" July 8, 1948.
"Grosberg Long Active in UJA (Aids Drive)," *The Schenectady Gazette*, [Schenectady, NY], Nov. 6, 1950 p. (unknown).
"Jewish Groups Will Hear Albany Prof," *The Schenectady Gazette*, [Schenectady, NY], May 26, 1952, p.22.
"Pledge Support to Council's Donor Plan Project Benefit," *The Schenectady Gazette*, [Schenectady, NY], Sept. 23, 1954.
"Joseph E. Grosberg To Be Feted June 30," *The Schenectady Gazette*, [Schenectady, NY], June 11, 1958.
"Israeli Aide Talks June 30 At Sch'dy," *Time's Union*, [Albany, NY], June 14, 1958, p.3.
Bolkosky Sidney M., Harmony & Dissonance: "Voices of Jewish Identity in Detroit," 1914-1967, pp 168-169.
"6 Sch'dy Jewish Leaders To Be 'Golden Honorees'," *The Schenectady Gazette*, [Schenectady, NY], Sept. 28, 1968, p.13.
"Introduction-Schenectady Jewish History," Schenectady County Historical Society, https://schenectadyhist.wordpress.com/2010/01/ Jan. 4, 2010.
"Gates of Heaven," Schenectady County Historical Society, https://schenectadyhist.wordpress.com/2010/01/ Jan 5, 2010.
"Beth Israel and Orthodox Congregations," Schenectady County Historical Society, https://schenectadyhist.wordpress.com/2010/01/ Jan 8, 2010.
"Jewish Businesses in Schenectady," Schenectady County Historical Society, https://schenectadyhist.wordpress.com/2010/01/ Jan 9, 2010.
"Organizations and Associations," Schenectady County Historical Society, https://schenectadyhist.wordpress.com/2010/01/ Jan 11, 2010.
"Kaddish For President Garfield," Schenectady County Historical Society, https://schenectadyhist.wordpress.com/2010/01/ Jan 12, 2010.

"World Community," Schenectady County Historical Society, https://schenectadyhist.wordpress.com/2010/01/ Jan 13, 2010.

Strum, Harvey, "Schenectady's Jews, Zionism and the Persecuted European Jews," New York History Review Press, 2019 Annual Issue, Vol 13, Issue 1, published January 11, 2020, pp.13-28.

United Hebrew Community

"Hebrew Community House is Opened," *The Schenectady Gazette*, [Schenectady, NY], June 15, 1923.

Newspaper Notice, Building Permit, *The Schenectady Gazette*, [Schenectady, NY], Oct. 14, 1924, p.6.

"Hebrew Societies Will Meet Tonight To Plan Building," *The Schenectady Gazette*, [Schenectady, NY], May 10, 1926, p.5.

"United Hebrew Community Does Good Work Here," *The Schenectady Gazette*, [Schenectady, NY], Apr. 30, 1926, p.10.

"Predict Increase in Regular Activities of Hebrew Associations," *The Schenectady Gazette*, [Schenectady, NY], Mar. 9, 1927, p.4.

"Grosberg Re-Elects Hebrew Group Head," *The Schenectady Gazette*, [Schenectady, NY], Apr. 14, 1928, p. (unknown).

United Synagogue of America

"Rally Planned At Synagogue," *Times Union*, [Albany, NY], Dec. 4, 1932.

"Jewry Moves to Strengthen Jewish Life," *The Schenectady Gazette*, [Schenectady, NY], Jan. 26, 1932, p.2.

"United Synagogue to Meet in Schenectady," *Jewish Daily Bulletin*, [New York, NY], Jan. 3, 1933, p.2.

"Region United Synagogue to Convene Here," *The Schenectady Gazette*, [Schenectady, NY], Jan. 20, 1933.

"Lurie Elected Head of United Jewish Group," *The Schenectady Gazette*, [Schenectady, NY], Jan. 23, 1933, p.9.

"A.D. Lurie Elected District President," *The Morning Herald*, [Gloversville and Johnstown, NY], Jan. 24, 1933.

Young Men's Hebrew Association (YMHA)

"Y.M.H.A. Formally Launched," *The American Jewish Chronicle*, July 21, 1916, p. 688.

"To Reorganize Club," *The Schenectady Gazette*, [Schenectady, NY], Aug. 4, 1916.

"Jews Unite With Enthusiasm for Local Y.M.H.A." *The Schenectady Gazette*, [Schenectady, NY], Sept. 23, 1916, p.2.

"Del Salmon to Act as Chairman, Plans for Organizing Young Men's Hebrew Assn. Going Forward Rapidly," *The Schenectady Gazette*, [Schenectady, NY], Sept. 21, 1916, p.2.

"Y.M.H.A. Meeting Tomorrow to be Largely Attended," *The Schenectady Gazette*, [Schenectady, NY], Sept. 23, 1916, p.3.

"Y.M.H.A. Formally Launched," *The American Jewish Chronicle*, Volume 1, Nov 3, 1916.

"Hebrew Orders To Meet," *The Schenectady Gazette*, [Schenectady, NY], Oct. 25, 1920, p.13.

"Y.M. and Y.W.H.A. to meet," *The Schenectady Gazette*, [Schenectady, NY], Nov 30, 1920, p.7.

"Y.M.H.A. to Celebrate Hanukah Sunday," *The Schenectady Gazette*, [Schenectady, NY], Dec. 7, 1923.

"Hebrew Clubs Have Eventful Year in City," *The Schenectady Gazette*, [Schenectady, NY], Dec. 31, 1923, p.9.

"Etkin Again Heads Y.M.H.A.," *The Schenectady Gazette*, [Schenectady, NY], Oct. 24, 1924, p.11.

"Y.M.H.A. Will Meet Tonight," *The Schenectady Gazette*, [Schenectady, NY], Dec. 15, 1924, p.7.

"Plans for Jewish Convention Made," *The Schenectady Gazette*, [Schenectady, NY], July 27, 1925, p.5.

"Simon Etkin Heads Y.M.H.A. for 1926," *The Schenectady Gazette*, [Schenectady, NY], Oct. 15, 1925, p.2.

"Judge Liddle Speaks to Y.M. and Y.W.H.A." *The Schenectady Gazette*, [Schenectady, NY], Apr. 9, 1926, p.6.

"Hebrew Premises Sold At Public Auction," *The Schenectady Gazette*, [Schenectady, NY], Mar. 25, 1929.

"Hebrew Community Holds Annual meeting and Elects Directors," *The Schenectady Gazette*, [Schenectady, NY], May 1, 1929.

"Given Re-elected Head of Y.M. and W.A. Federation," *Albany Times Union*, [Albany, NY], date (unknown)1929 p. (unknown).

"Given Re-elected as State Jewish Head," *Syracuse Journal*, [Syracuse, NY], May 31, 1929, p.8.

"Jewish Center Auxiliary Has Anniversary," *The Schenectady Gazette*, [Schenectady, NY], Feb. 22, 1933, p.11.

"Enroll 38 in Center Drive," *The Schenectady Gazette*, [Schenectady, NY], Apr. 3, 1935, p.2.

"Jewish Groups Pick Delegates," *The Schenectady Gazette*, [Schenectady, NY], Dec 17, 1936, p.(unknown).

"Committee Heads Named," *The Schenectady Gazette*, [Schenectady, NY], Aug. 29, 1940, p.7.

Zionist Activities and Moriah Zionist Association

"Zionist Plan Dance," *The Schenectady Gazette*, [Schenectady, NY], Oct. 2, 1914.

"Dance to Assist War Sufferers and Library," *The Schenectady Gazette*, [Schenectady, NY], Sept. 21, 1914, p.3.

"Officers of Zion-Lodge, No. 909, I.O.O.F., Seated," *The Schenectady Gazette*, [Schenectady, NY], Jan. 9, 1915, p.8.

"Food Certain to Reach Palestine," *The Schenectady Gazette*, [Schenectady, NY], Feb. 23, 1915, p.4.

"Rabbi Jacobs to Talk to Zionists Tonight," *The Schenectady Gazette*, [Schenectady, NY], Mar. 22, 1915, p.8.

"Zionists Elect Delegates," *American Jewish Chronicle*, May 11, 1917, p.223.

"Zion Lodge to Celebrate Its 10th Anniversary," *The Schenectady Gazette*, [Schenectady, NY], June 19, 1917, p.2.

"Local Zionists to Attend Conference," *The Schenectady Gazette*, [Schenectady, NY], Nov. 23, 1925, p.12.

"Zionist Leader Coming Here," Times-Union, [Albany, NY], Dec. 17, 1926, p.(unknown).

"Local Men Designated to Welcome Weizmann," *The Schenectady Gazette*, [Schenectady, NY], Jan 8, 1927, p.18.
"Palestine Rift Healed, Local Zionists Learn," *The Schenectady Gazette*, [Schenectady, NY], Mar. 10, 1927, p.11.
"Zion Lodge Entertains Campbell at Past Noble Grands Night Meeting," *The Schenectady Gazette*, [Schenectady, NY], Feb. 24, 1928, p.4.
"Open Campaign to Raise $7,000 for Palestine Appeal," *The Schenectady Gazette*, [Schenectady, NY], Apr. 23, 1928, p.3.
"Zion Lodge Will Hold 3rd Past Grands' Night," *The Schenectady Gazette*, [Schenectady, NY], Mar. 26, 1930, p.14.
"Zion Lodge to Hold Past Grands' Night," *The Schenectady Gazette*, [Schenectady, NY], Apr. 22, 1931, p.7.
"Zion Lodge to Observe 27th Anniversary," *The Schenectady Gazette*, [Schenectady, NY], Mar. date (unknown) 1934, p. (unknown).
"Zion I.O.O.F. Lodge Marks Anniversary," *The Schenectady Gazette*, [Schenectady, NY], 1934 date (unknown), p.(unknown).
"Zion Lodge to Observe 27th Anniversary," *The Schenectady Gazette*, [Schenectady, NY], 1934 date (unknown), p.(unknown).
"Grosberg to Tell Local Zionists of Trip to Holy Land," *The Schenectady Gazette*, [Schenectady, NY], Apr. 19, 1935, p.20.
"Vice President, Joseph E. Grosberg" (photo), *The Schenectady Gazette*, [Schenectady, NY], June 18, 1940, p.7.
"Dr. Green Will Address Zionist Group, *The Schenectady Gazette*, [Schenectady, NY], Nov 6, 1942.
"Rabbi Bloom Will Address Zionists Here," *The Schenectady Gazette*, [Schenectady, NY], June 6, 1946, p. 10.
Donger, Sundel (ed.) "The Jewish National Fund," A Zionist Primer: Essays by Various Writers.
"Local Zionists Will Install Area Officers," *The Schenectady Gazette*, [Schenectady, NY], June 4, 1947, p.7.
"Asks for Mass Action on UN Zionist Report," *The Schenectady Gazette*, [Schenectady, NY], Oct. 4, 1947, p.22.
"Local Zionists Will Install Area Officers," *The Schenectady Gazette*, [Schenectady, NY], June 4, 1947, p.7.
"Rally Salutes New State of Israel," (photo) *The Schenectady Gazette*, [Schenectady, NY], date (unknown) 1948, p. (unknown).

Civic Activities References

Businessmen Association

"Business Men Will Organize to Improve Traffic Conditions," *The Schenectady Gazette*, [Schenectady, NY], Apr. 3, 1925, p.14.
"Traffic Improvement Association Meets," *The Schenectady Gazette*, [Schenectady, NY], Apr. 10, 1926, p.10.

Chamber of Commerce

"Chamber's 200 Army Rapidly Being Filled," *The Schenectady Gazette*, [Schenectady, NY], Sept.16, 1925, p.8.
"Chamber of Commerce Membership Campaign Nets 451 on First Day, *The Schenectady Gazette*, [Schenectady, NY], Sept. 23, 1925, p. (unknown).
"Ballots Pour in for Election Chamber of Commerce Officers, *The Schenectady Gazette*, [Schenectady, NY], Sept. 20, 1927.
"Chamber of Commerce Membership Campaign Nets 451 On First Day," *The Schenectady Gazette*, [Schenectady, NY], Sept. 23, 1925, p. (unknown).
"Company President Addresses Grocers," *The Morning Herald*, [Gloversville and Johnstown, NY], Nov. 11, 1930, p. 12.
"Commerce Body Names Committees for Year," *The Schenectady Gazette*, [Schenectady, NY], Oct. 29, 1938, p.7.
"C. of C. Appoints Groups to 'Keep This City Ahead'," *The Schenectady Gazette*, [Schenectady, NY], Jan. 8, 1941, p.2.

Charity Drives

"Merchants to Promote Sale of War Bonds," *The Schenectady Gazette*, [Schenectady, NY], May 25, 1917, p. 4.
"Funds for Seals Rapidly Climb," *The Schenectady Gazette*, [Schenectady, NY], Dec. 13, 1919, p.7.
"Announces Gifts to Humane Shelter," *The Schenectady Gazette*, [Schenectady, NY], Dec. 10, 1920, p.21.
"Donation List of Humane Society Has Many Names," *The Schenectady Gazette*, [Schenectady, NY], Aug. 1, 1923, p.5.
"Donors to Humane Society Are Listed," *The Schenectady Gazette*, [Schenectady, NY], Jan. 17, 1924.
"Large Number Respond to Call from "Y" to Serve in Campaign, *The Schenectady Gazette*, [Schenectady, NY], Oct. 3, 1925, p.20.
"$100,000 Is Needed to Provide for Needy Here," *The Schenectady Gazette*, [Schenectady, NY], Dec 2, 1930, p.1.
"Warm Clothing Is Sought for Needy in City," *The Schenectady Gazette*, [Schenectady, NY], Feb. 4, 1931, p.24.
"More Donations to Relief Fund Listed," *The Schenectady Gazette*, [Schenectady, NY], Jan. 5, 1931.
"Special Gifts Group Named," *The Schenectady Gazette*, [Schenectady, NY], Apr. 20, 1940, p.22.
"List Workers for Banking Division of 7th War Loan," *The Schenectady Gazette*, [Schenectady, NY], May 12, 1945, p.7.
"Pulling Heads Negro College Fund Drive," *The Schenectady Gazette*, [Schenectady, NY], May 22, 1947, p.10.

Community Chest

"Welfare Organizations Put O.K. on Community Chest After Year's Use," *The Schenectady Gazette*, [Schenectady, NY], May 7, 1925, p.12.
"Committee on Special Gifts for Campaign of Chest Is Designated, *The Schenectady Gazette*, [Schenectady, NY], Apr. 24, 1930, p.16.
"Special Gifts Committee of Chest Named, "*The Schenectady Gazette*, [Schenectady, NY], Apr. 17, 1933
"Heads War Chest," *The Schenectady Gazette*, [Schenectady, NY], March 21, 1942, p.24.
"H.R. KinKaid Community Chest President," *The Schenectady Gazette*, [Schenectady, NY], Feb. 19, 1944, p.9.
"Sherry Named Community Chest Head," *The Schenectady Gazette*, [Schenectady, NY], Feb. 17, 1945, p.9.
"Chest Drive Special Gifts Group Named," *The Schenectady Gazette*, [Schenectady, NY], (date unknown) 1945, p.(unknown).
"Chest Again Elects Ruvin As President," *The Schenectady Gazette*, [Schenectady, NY], Feb. 22, 1947, s.2, p.1.
"Busy Week Ahead for Chest Drive," *The Schenectady Gazette*, [Schenectady, NY], Sept. 21, 1948, p12.

County Civil Defense & Citizen Unity Committee

"Defense League Fund Now Nears The $800 Mark," *The Schenectady Gazette*, [Schenectady, NY], May 19, 1917, p. 2.
"Supervisors to Meet Tuesday," *The Schenectady Gazette*, [Schenectady, NY], July 6, 1917, p.9.
"Business Men Offer Help to Defense League," *The Schenectady Gazette*, [Schenectady, NY], May 18, 1917, p.8.
"Jos. Grosberg Appointed CD Food Chief," *The Schenectady Gazette*, [Schenectady, NY], July 19, 1954, p.13.
"Area Food Supplies Briefed on Plans To Work with CD Units in Emergency," *The Schenectady Gazette*, [Schenectady, NY], Oct. 14, 1952, p.7.

Elks

"Elect Officers at Elks' Lodge," *The Schenectady Gazette*, [Schenectady, NY], Mar. 12, 1919, p.16.
"Elks Lodge to Honor 'Old Timers' Today," *The Schenectady Gazette*, [Schenectady, NY], Oct. 25. 1949.
"Elks Club to Hold Annual Jewish Night," *The Schenectady Gazette*, [Schenectady, NY], Nov. 28, 1944, p.11.

Ellis Hospital

"Hospital Lists New System for Visitors," *The Schenectady Gazette*, [Schenectady, NY], June 12, 1945, s2, p.1.

Emergency Welfare Services/War Price and Rationing Board

"Schenectadians Need Have No Fear," *The Schenectady Gazette*, [Schenectady, NY], Nov. 5, 1942, p.19.
"Price Control Panel to Hear OPA Speaker," *The Schenectady Gazette*, [Schenectady, NY], June 2, 1943, p.9.
"Food Situation To Be Discussed At Hotel Today," *The Schenectady Gazette*, [Schenectady, NY], Nov. 9, 1943, p.20.
"Plan Weekly Price Survey," *The Schenectady Gazette*, [Schenectady, NY], July 8, 1944, p.9.

Kiwanis

"Kiwanis Club Holds Its First Luncheon," *The Schenectady Gazette*, [Schenectady, NY], May 22, 1919
"Kiwanians Indorse Quinlivan Fund and "Y" Building Drive," *The Schenectady Gazette*, [Schenectady, NY], Sept. 17, 1925, p.12.
"Kiwanians Out in Force to Sell Paper, 'Kiwanis Kapers'," *The Schenectady Gazette*, [Schenectady, NY], Apr. 20, 1926, p.12.
"Kiwanis to Hear Lynch," *The Schenectady Gazette*, [Schenectady, NY], Nov. 18, 1930, p.11.
"Begley, Wolcott on State Bodies of Kiwanis Club," *The Schenectady Gazette*, [Schenectady, NY], Nov. 21, 1932, p.2.
"Kiwanians to Stage Benefit Bridge Party (at Silver Slipper), *The Schenectady Gazette* [Schenectady, NY], Apr. 6, 1933, p.20.
"Hold Kiwanis Party Tonight," (at Silver Slipper), *The Schenectady Gazette* [Schenectady, NY], Apr. 25, 1933, p.2.
"Kiwanis Host To Dr. Carroll," *The Schenectady Gazette*, [Schenectady, NY], May 14, 1935, p. 22.
"Kiwanis Board Decides 'Buddy' Camp Project," *The Schenectady Gazette*, [Schenectady, NY], May 15, 1935, p.2.
"District Governor To Seat Kiwanis Officers," *The Schenectady Gazette*, [Schenectady, NY], Dec. 28, 1935, p. 5.
"Kiwanians to Provide Camp Vacation for 170 Boys and Girls," *The Schenectady Gazette*), [Schenectady, NY], May 20, 1937, p.28.
"Kiwanis Group Inspects Camp at Mariaville," *The Schenectady Gazette*, [Schenectady, NY], Aug. 5, 1937, p.21.
"Kiwanis Club to Hear Medical Society Officer," *The Schenectady Gazette,* [Schenectady, NY], Oct. 12, 1937, p.8.
"Slate Kelly to Head Kiwanis," *The Schenectady Gazette*, [Schenectady, NY], Oct. 28, 1937, p.2.
"Name Kiwanis 1939 Chairman of Committees," *The Schenectady Gazette*, [Schenectady, NY], Dec. 10, 1938, p. (unknown).
"Kiwanians to Dispense Christmas Cheer to 1,000 Persons," *The Schenectady Gazette*, [Schenectady, NY], Dec. 22, 1938, p.17.
"President-Elect Picks Kiwanis Committees," *The Schenectady Gazette*, [Schenectady, NY], Dec. 22, 1938, p.9.

"Grosberg Wins Golf Trophy in Kiwanians Test," *The Schenectady Gazette*, [Schenectady, NY], Aug. 25, 1939, p.32.
"Kiwanians Plan Camp Projects," *The Schenectady Gazette*, [Schenectady, NY], May 18, 1939, p.28.
"Kiwanis to Hear Minister Speak," *The Schenectady Gazette*, [Schenectady, NY], Nov. 20, 1939, p.20.
"City Kiwanians Pick Grosberg To Head Club Gazette," *The Schenectady Gazette*, [Schenectady, NY], November 9, 1939, p.6.
"Cliffe Talks to Kiwanis Unit on Social Security," *The Schenectady Gazette*, [Schenectady, NY], Dec. 7, 1939, p.9.
"Kiwanis to Hear About Hospital," *The Schenectady Gazette*, [Schenectady, NY], Dec. 11, 1939, p.14.
"Committees for '40 Are Picked by Kiwanis Club," *The Schenectady Gazette*, [Schenectady, NY], Jan. 4, 1940, p.5.
"City Club Marks Founding Of Kiwanis International," *The Schenectady Gazette*, [Schenectady, NY], Jan. 25, 1940, p.3.
"Kiwanis Club To Install 1937 Heads Tonight," *The Schenectady Gazette*, [Schenectady, NY], date (unknown), 1937, p.(unknown).
"Kiwanis Club to Mark 25th Anniversary," *The Schenectady Gazette*, [Schenectady, NY], Jan. 22, 1940, p.16.
"Kiwanis Hears Prof Bronner," *The Schenectady Gazette*, [Schenectady, NY], Feb. 15, 1940, p.22.
"Olft Addresses Kiwanis Club, *The Schenectady Gazette*, [Schenectady, NY], Apr. 4, 1940, p.15.
"170 Kiwanians Hear Godsen at Inter-Club Meet," *The Schenectady Gazette*, [Schenectady, NY], Apr. 18, 1940, p.5.
"Kiwanians to See Movies," *The Schenectady Gazette*, [Schenectady, NY], Apr. 22, 1940, p.3.
"Mariner Tells of Gov't Costs," *The Schenectady Gazette*, [Schenectady, NY], May 2, 1940, p.28.
"Local Kiwanis Golfers Best in Area Matches," *The Schenectady Gazette*, [Schenectady, NY], Aug. 22, 1940, p.21.
"City Club Marks Founding of Kiwanis International," *The Schenectady Gazette*, [Schenectady, NY], Jan. 25, 1940, p.3.
"Welcomes Kiwanis Governor," (photo) *The Schenectady Gazette*, [Schenectady, NY], Aug. 9, 1940, p.28.
"Warren Hill, Grosberg to Attend Parley," *The Schenectady Gazette*, [Schenectady, NY], June 18, 1940, p.2.
"Kiwanis Club to Stage Armistice Play at Meeting," *The Times Record*, [Troy, NY], Nov. 5, 1940, p.3.
"Service Clubs Hear Talk by Gipsy Smith," *The Schenectady Gazette*, [Schenectady, NY], Nov. 7, 1940, p.5.
"Kiwanis Club Seats Staff, Appoints 1941 Committees," *The Schenectady Gazette*, [Schenectady, NY], Jan. 13, 1941, p.4.
"Kiwanis Participate in Quiz Program, *The Schenectady Gazette*, [Schenectady, NY], Apr. 16, 1942, p.15.
"Kiwanians End Successful War Bond Drive," (photo) *The Schenectady Gazette*, [Schenectady, NY], Apr. 23, 1943.
"Kiwanis, Will Seat Officers Tomorrow," *The Schenectady Gazette*, [Schenectady, NY], Jan. 4, 1944, p. 16.
"Kiwanis Club Pays Tribute To Charter Members," (photo) *The Schenectady Gazette*, [Schenectady, NY], May 30, 1944, p.2.
"17 Honored on Kiwanis Club Anniversary," *Ibid.*
"Kiwanis Club Membership Reaches 105," *The Schenectady Gazette*, [Schenectady, NY], Jan. 4, 1945, p.18.
"Kiwanis Club Committees For 1946 Are Appointed," *The Schenectady Gazette*, [Schenectady, NY], Jan. 3, 1946, p.3.
"45 Children Feted at Party by Kiwanis," *The Schenectady Gazette*, [Schenectady, NY], July 12, 1946, p.24.
"Kiwanis to Honor Past Presidents," *The Schenectady Gazette*, [Schenectady, NY], June 2, 1948, p.10.
"Kiwanians Live UP to Name and More; Make Genuine Contribution to Nation," *The Schenectady Gazette*, [Schenectady, NY], Dec. 3, 1948, p.14.
"Charter Members of Local Kiwanis Club," *The Schenectady Gazette*, [Schenectady, NY], Dec. 3, 1948, p.14.
"Outside Work on Boys' Club Home Finished," *The Schenectady Gazette*, [Schenectady, NY], date (unknown), 1952, p.(unknown).
"Kiwanis Club Group Holds Fishing Junket, Picnic for 29 Boys," *The Schenectady Gazette*, [Schenectady, NY] Aug. 2, 1952, p.4.
"They're Off to Saratoga," (photo) *The Schenectady Gazette*, [Schenectady, NY], Aug. 17, 1953, p.12
"Kids Think Show's the Thing" (photo), *The Schenectady Gazette*, [Schenectady, NY], Sept. 8, 1953, p.10.
"Enjoying the Schenectady Kiwanis Club's First Annual Buffet," (photo) *The Schenectady Gazette*, [Schenectady, NY], Aug. 22, 1954, p.18.
"50 Youngsters Kiwanis Guests At Stage Play," *The Schenectady Gazette*, [Schenectady, NY], Aug. 6, 1955, p.9.
Lee, Everett S., The Story of The Kiwanis Club of Schenectady, New York, Kiwanis Club of Schenectady, 1964.

Saratoga Springs Cure and Convalescent Home

"Grosberg Is Made Director of Spa Home," *The Schenectady Gazette*, [Schenectady, NY], May 20, 1931.
"Name Saratoga Home Changed to Cure," *Ballston Spa Daily Journal*, [Ballston, NY], Apr. 28, 1933.
"17 Patients Now at Judea Home in Jefferson St.", *The Saratogian*, [Saratoga Springs, NY], Jun 2, 1932, p.3.
"Judea Home Closed," *The Saratogian*, [Saratoga Springs, NY], Sept 9 1932, p.5.

Seaboard Food Service

"Grosberg Food Service Chief," *The Schenectady Gazette*, [Schenectady, NY], June 20, 1936, p.7.

Schenectady Food Distributors' Council

"Local Food Distributors Form Council," *The Schenectady Gazette*, [Schenectady, NY], June 10, 1943, p.13.

Shaker Ridge Country Club
"Work Begun on New Club," *Albany Times-Union*, [Albany, NY], (date unknown) 1929, p.2.
"Shaker Ridge Events," *Albany Times-Union*, [Albany, NY], July (day unknown) 1946, p. (unknown).

St. Claire's Catholic Hospital

"New Hospital Plans to be Discussed Mon," *The Schenectady Gazette*, [Schenectady, NY], June 12 1945, s.2, p.1.
"$1,200,000 For Catholic Hospital Sought," *The Schenectady Gazette*, [Schenectady, NY], Aug. 1, 1945, p. 20.
"300 Pledge Support for Catholic Hospital," *The Schenectady Gazette*, [Schenectady, NY], June 19, 1945, s.2, p.1.
"Schenectady Civic Leaders Back Plan for New Hospital," The Evangelist [Albany, NY], June 22, 1945, p.3.
"Schenectady Leaders Lend Help to Drive for Catholic Hospital," The Evangelist [Albany, NY], Aug 10, 1945, p.1,3.
"Hospital's Dedication Today Marks Realization of Dream of 30 Years," *The Schenectady Gazette*, [Schenectady, NY], Aug. 12, 1949, p.21.

Taxpayers' Association

"Government Must Gauge Costs On Ability of Taxpayers to Pay," *The Schenectady Gazette*, [Schenectady, NY], Apr. 13, 1934, p.19.

Miscellaneous
"Annual Pilgrimage of Supreme Orient Brings Over 5,000," (Oriental Order of Humility and Perfection, i.e. Shriners) *The Schenectady Gazette*, [Schenectady, NY], Aug. 15, 1919, p.11.
"Mill Employee Hurt," *The Schenectady Gazette*, [Schenectady, NY], Feb 4, 1919, p. 5.
"Joseph E. Grosberg Will Speak at Junior League," *The Schenectady Gazette*, [Schenectady, NY], Nov. 26, 1925, p. (unknown).
"David Weiss Plays Tonight at Chapel of Union College," *The Schenectady Gazette*, [Schenectady, NY], Apr. 20, 1926, p.12.
"Long House, Tent Third of Mile in Length, Ordered for 9-Day Jubilee Here in June," (Joe committee for Gateway Celebration) *The Schenectady Gazette*, [Schenectady, NY], Apr. 29 1926, p.4.
"Scout Pow Wow Plans Will Be Discussed at Big Meeting Tonight," (Joe member at large to Schenectady Council) *The Schenectady Gazette*, [Schenectady, NY], Jan. 26, 1927, p.11.
Newspaper Notice, Confirmed Commissioner of Deeds, City of Troy, *The Troy Times*, [Troy, NY], May 13, 1928.
"As Store Employees Celebrated on Thanksgiving Eve," (photo) *The Schenectady Gazette*, [Schenectady, NY], Nov. 29, 1930, p.6.
"Rabbi Freedman Installed as Spiritual Leader Here," *Amsterdam Daily Democrat and Recorder*, [Amsterdam, NY], Oct. 5, 1931, p. (unknown).
Newspaper Notice, Named Commissioner of Deeds, *The Troy Times*, [Troy, NY], May 20, 1932, p.14.
Newspaper Notice, Confirmed Commissioner of Deeds for City of Troy, *The Troy Times*, [Troy, NY], June 1, 1932, p.9.
"Scout Council Names Peter Wold Head For 4th Consecutive Year," *The Schenectady Gazette*, [Schenectady, NY], 1934 date (unknown).
"Apex Store Marks Close of Buyers' Sale," *The Schenectady Gazette*, [Schenectady, NY], May 12, 1937.
"Mrs. B.M. Mills Elected Head of Girls' Club Unit," (Joe director), *The Schenectady Gazette*, [Schenectady, NY], Apr. 4, 1939, p.7.
"Flag Day Ceremony Set Tonight," *The Schenectady Gazette*, [Schenectady, NY], June 14, 1940, p.3.
"Food Industry Group Protests Point Rationing," *The Schenectady Gazette*, [Schenectady, NY], Feb. 25, 1943, p.8.
"Point Rationing Is Discussed," *The Schenectady Gazette*, [Schenectady, NY], Mar. 1, 1943, p.4.
"Cleaning, Laundering Concern Purchases Sycaway Property," *The Troy Times*, [Troy, NY], Jan. 19, 1952, p.7.

Personal Life References

Home Life, Anniversary, Obituaries, Etc.

"Betrothal Announced," (Joe attends out-of-town wedding), *Morning Star*, [Glens Falls, NY], Oct. 27, 1904, p.6.
"Friends Entertained," (… "congratulate Mr. Grosberg on his recovery from a long illness"), *The Schenectady Gazette*, [Schenectady, NY], May 12, 1914. p. (unknown).
Classified Ad, "Girl Wanted for Housework," *The Schenectady Gazette*, [Schenectady, NY], Nov. 12, 1914, p.9.
"Equity Calendar Will Be Called Tomorrow Noon" (verdict in favor of J.E. Grosberg), *The Schenectady Gazette*, [Schenectady, NY], Feb. 26, 1918.
"Grocery Chain Head Who Leaves for South," *The Schenectady Gazette*, [Schenectady, NY], Feb. 9, 1931, p.6.
"Observe Silver Wedding Anniversary," *The Schenectady Gazette*, [Schenectady, NY], Nov. 4, 1931, p.6.
"Return Home," (from trip to Detroit) *The Schenectady Gazette*, [Schenectady, NY], July 13, 1933, p.11.
"Reception Tonight," (Lifschitz hold party for Grosbergs who are leaving on a cruise), *The Schenectady Gazette*, [Schenectady, NY], Feb. 11, 1935, p.13.
Passenger List, *S.S. Rex*, Joseph and Rae Grosberg, Mar. 1935.
"To Sail Wednesday," (trip to Egypt, Spain, Palestine, and France), *The Schenectady Gazette*, [Schenectady, NY], Dec. 12, 1935, p.11.

"Police Investigate Two Burglaries," *The Schenectady Gazette*, [Schenectady, NY], (date unknown) 1935, p. (unknown).
"Kappa Nu," (Grosbergs chaperone dance) *The Concordiensis*, Union College, [Schenectady, NY], May 13, 1938, p. 6.
"Tea Dansant," *Times-Union*, [Albany, NY], June 25, 1938, p.22.
"Social Service Group Honors Mrs. Grosberg," *The Schenectady Gazette*, [Schenectady, NY], Nov. 25, 1943, p.22.
"Mr., Mrs. J.E. Grosberg Celebrate 60th Anniversary," *The Schenectady Gazette*, [Schenectady, NY], Oct. 17, 1966, p.19.
"The Sixtieth," Knickerbocker Social Whirl, *Knickerbocker News*, [Albany, NY], Oct. 25, 1966, p.7B.
"J.E. Grosberg Dies," *Niagara Gazette*, [Niagara Falls, NY], July 27, 1970.
"Joseph J. (*sic*) Grosberg, Area Supermarket Pioneer, Dies," *The Times Record*, [Troy, NY], July 27, 1970, p.3.
"Joseph Grosberg Death," *New York Times*, [New York, NY], July 27, 1970.
"J.E. Grosberg Dies; Supermarket Head", *The Schenectady Gazette*, [Schenectady, NY], July 27, 1970, p.21.
"Joseph E. Grosberg, Central Markets Founder, Succumbs," *Amsterdam Evening Recorder*, [Amsterdam, NY], July 27, 1970, Sec. 2, p.9.
"Grosberg, Area Market Chain Founder, Dies at 86," *The Leader-Herald*, [Gloversville - Johnstown, NY], July 27, 1970, p.11.
"Grosberg, Market Founder, Dead at 86," *Times-Union*, [Albany, NY] July 27, 1970, p.6.
"Grosberg, Pioneer In Super Markets," *Knickerbocker News*, [Albany, NY], July 27, 1970, p.12C.
"Joseph E. Grosberg Dies in Florida," *Post-Star*, [Glens Falls, NY], July 28, 1970, p.5.
"Mrs. Rae Grosberg Dies," *The Schenectady Gazette*, [Schenectady, NY], Nov. 8, 1971. p. (unknown).

Grosberg Relatives

"The Magistrate's Hour," Jacob Grosberg Wine Stolen, *Troy Daily Times*, [Troy, NY], 1893.
"The Magistrate's Hour," Jacob Grosberg Assault, *Troy Daily Times*, [Troy, NY] Sept. 17, 1896.
"Will Give Dinner in Honor of Meyer (*sic*) Grosberg," *The Schenectady Gazette*, [Schenectady, NY], June 9, 1915, p.10.
"Amateur Baseball" (Benjamin Grosberg), *The Schenectady Gazette*, [Schenectady, NY], Sept. 20, 1912, p.2.
History of the Class of 1912, (Myer Grosberg) Yale College - Volume 1 - p. 365.
"Miss Englebardt Entertains," (Harold and Benjamin Grosberg guests), *The Schenectady Gazette*, [Schenectady, NY], Nov. 13, 1914, p.5.
"Officers Elected," (Myer Groserg in Zionist group), *The Schenectady Gazette*, [Schenectady, NY], Jan. 28, 1914, p.5.
"Personals," (William Grosberg leaves for Detroit), *The Schenectady Gazette*, [Schenectady, NY], Dec. 12, 1914, p.4.
"Jews to Sell Flags For Palestine Fund," (Myer Grosberg) *The Schenectady Gazette*, [Schenectady, NY], Feb. 25, 1915, p.3.
"Busy Program of Union Festivities Brought to Close," (Myer Grosberg) *The Schenectady Gazette*, [Schenectady, NY], June 10, 1915, p.3.
Engagement Announcement (William Grosberg and Rose Morris), *The Schenectady Gazette*, [Schenectady, NY], Sept. 11, 1917, p.12.
"Weddings: Grosberg-Morris," *The Schenectady Gazette*, [Schenectady, NY], June 11, 1918, p.10.
Directory of American Association of Engineers (Morris Greenblath), 1918 – 1919.
Wedding Announcement, Kaufman-Greenblath, *The Schenectady Gazette*, [Schenectady, NY], July 6, 1922, p.8.
"Lack of Safety Gate on Lift is Cause of Death," (of Harry Morris), *The Schenectady Gazette*, [Schenectady, NY], Jan. 9, 1925, p. 12.
"Local Firm is Chartered," (William Grosberg in business with Solomon Morris), *The Schenectady Gazette*, [Schenectady, NY], Mar. 4, 1926, p12.
"Papers of Incorporation," (William Grosberg in business with Solomon Morris), *The Schenectady Gazette*, [Schenectady, NY], Mar. 6, 1926.
"Blossom Heath, Dance Hall on Albany Road, Is Destroyed by Fire," *The Schenectady Gazette*, [Schenectady, NY], Aug. 8, 1928.
"Cause of Blossom Heath Fire Sought By State Trooper," *The Schenectady Gazette*, [Schenectady, NY], Aug. 9, 1928, p.2.
"7 Held in Rum Exchange Raid," (Harry Grosberg), Detroit Free Press, [Detroit, MI], Dec. 4, 1929.
"All Licenses Are Returned," (William Grosberg) The *Morning Herald*, [Gloversville-Johnstown, NY], Feb. 3, 1930, p.2.
"Grosberg Leaves Employ of S. Morris and Sons," (William Grosberg), *The Schenectady Gazette*, [Schenectady, NY], Feb. 20, 1930, p.11.
"Mrs. J. Grosberg Dies At Detroit," *The Schenectady Gazette*, [Schenectady, NY], date (unknown) 1934, p.(unknown).
Death Notice, Anna Grosberg, *Detroit Jewish Chronicle*, [Detroit, MI], Dec. 7, 1934.
Foreclosure Notice (Harry and Benjamin Grosberg), *The Enterprise*, [Altamont, NY], NY, Aug. 9, 1935, p.8.
Foreclosure Notice (Harry and Benjamin Grosberg), *The Enterprise*, [Altamont, NY], Aug. 23, 1935, p.11.
Death Notice, Rebecca Greenberg, *The Times Record*, [Troy, NY], Nov. 5, 1936, p.11.
Death Notice, Jennie Esther Greenblath, *The Times Record*, [Troy, NY], June 5, 1940, p.13.

Obituary, Mrs. Morris Greenblath, *The Times Record*, [Troy, NY], June 5, 1940, p.2.
Obituary, Morris Greenblath, *The Schenectady Gazette*, [Schenectady, NY], June 17, 1943, p.13.
Death Notice, Morris Greenblath, *The Times Record*, [Troy, NY], June 16, 1943.
"5 Children Share Estate" (Morris Greenblath) *Times Union*, [Albany, NY], June 25, 1943, p.12.
"File Tax Reports on Three Estates in Probate Court," (Morris Greenblath Estate), *The Times Record*, [Troy, NY], Aug. 24, 1943, p.2.
Notice of Unveiling of Greenblath monument, *The Times Record*, [Troy, NY], June 9, 1944, p.13.
"Mrs. Engle, 87, Dies; Funeral To Be Today," *The Schenectady Gazette*, [Schenectady, NY], (date unknown) 1957, p. (unknown).
Death Notice, Mrs. Hannah Engle, *Times Union*, [Albany, NY], Jan. 23, 1957, p.32.
Death Notice, Mrs. Hannah Engle, *The Schenectady Gazette*, [Schenectady, NY], Jan. 23, 1957.
Obituary, Hannah Engle, *The Times Record*, [Troy, NY], Jan. 2,1 1957, p. 22.
Bellin, Mildred Grosberg, "Rosh Hashanah, 5719," *Gourmet Magazine*, Sep. 1958, p.26-27, 56-58.
"Trot Owner's License Revoked," (Benjamin Grosberg), *Long Island Star-Journal*, [Long Island City, New York] Jan. 9, 1959, p. 15.
Champagne, Marian, Quimby and Son, The Bobbs-Merrill Company, Inc., New York, 1962.
"Rose Grosberg Dies; Was Jewish Leader," *The Detroit Jewish News,* [Detroit, MI], April 24, 1964, p.30.
"Charles Grosberg, Supermarket Pioneer, Marks 80th Birthday," *Detroit Jewish News,* [Detroit, MI], Sept. 17, 1965, p.26.
"Charles Grosberg, Philanthropist, National Leader in Israel Bond Drives, Dies in Florida, Aged 83," *The Detroit Jewish News*, [Detroit, MI] Dec. 27, 1968, p.9.
Obituary, Mayer L. Cramer, *Amsterdam Evening Recorder*, [Amsterdam, NY], Feb. 9, 1970, s.2, p.9.
Death Notice Mayer L. Cramer, *Times-Union*, [Albany, NY], Feb. 10, 1970, p. (unknown).
Grosberg, Merwin, "Charles Grosberg: a Supermarket Pioneer," *Michigan Jewish History,* The Jewish Historical Society of Michigan, Vol. 25, No. 1-2, 1985, pp. 6-9.
"Mrs. Grosberg, Native of City," (Harold Grosberg's wife Dorothy) *The Schenectady Gazette*, [Schenectady, NY], Jan. 16, 1986.
Porter, Peg, "Lost Business of Ypsilanti...Packers Outlet," *Ypsilanti Gleanings*, Spring 2011, pp. 3, 22-23.

Misc. Grosberg Records

Ship Records for Chane, Josch, and Chaskel Grosberg, Aug. 31, 1887, CastleGarden.org.
Draft Registration Card for Joseph Ezikial Grosberg, Schenectady, NY, Serial Number 2111, Order Number 277, Sept. 12, 1918.
Draft Registration Card for Benjamin Grosberg, Detroit, Michigan, No. 114, date (unknown).
Draft Registration Card for Charles Grosberg, Detroit, Michigan, Serial Number 696, date (unknown).
Draft Registration Card for Harry Louis Grosberg, Detroit, Michigan, Serial Number 1290, Order Number 1932, date (unknown).
Draft Registration Card for Myer Grosberg, Detroit, Michigan, No. 18.T. date (unknown).
Draft Registration Card for Wm. Grosberg, Detroit, Michigan, No. 45(digit illegible) date (unknown).
Death Certificate for Anna Lasky Grosberg, Michigan Department of Health, Wayne County, Detroit, Michigan, State Office No 188925, Dec. 1, 1934.
Death Certificate for Jacob Grosberg, Michigan Department of Health, Wayne County, Detroit, Michigan, Apr. 29, 1946.

Associates

Classified Ad, (Golub and Putterman Wholesale Grocers selling two horses), *The Schenectady Gazette*, [Schenectady, NY], Aug. 10, 1915, p.15.
Classified Ad, Golub Wholesale Selling two horses, *The Schenectady Gazette*, [Schenectady, NY], June 9, 1920.
"Vicinity Stores Included in Big Merger of Shops," (Hugh R. Mccarney) *The Saratogian*, [Saratoga Springs, NY], Oct. 3, 1925, p.8.
"Levines Observe 18th Wedding Anniversary," *The Schenectady Gazette*, [Schenectady, NY], Feb. 10, 1937, p.15.
"The Levines Mark 50th Anniversary," *The Schenectady Gazette*, [Schenectady, NY], June 9, 1969, p.18.
"Levine Noble Grand of Zion Lodge, I.O.O.F.," *The Schenectady Gazette*, [Schenectady, NY], Dec. 31, 1914, p.3.
"Nathan Levine, Managed Store," (Obituary), *The Schenectady Gazette*, [Schenectady, NY], Feb. 12, 1985, p.25.
"Schenectady Firm Changes Hands" (Mayer Cramer, president of Mohawk Gas & Oil Corp. firm to retire), *Knickerbocker News*, [Albany, NY], Feb. 16, 1953, p.14-B.

www.ingramcontent.com/pod-product-compliance
Lightning Source LLC
LaVergne TN
LVHW061249100826
845148LV00008B/1071